# AN EASY BOOK TO HAPPINESS

## HOW TO GET RID OF BAGGAGE AND ACHIEVE ONE'S OWN GOALS

by Maria Beatrice Alonzi

YOU CAN FIND ME HERE:
**website**: mariabeatrice.com
**Italian verified Instagram Profile**: @mariabeatrice
**New English Instagram Profile**: @mariabeatricealonzi

*To you, who believe that all is lost or has already been written and, despite this, you are ready to change.*

# CONTENTS

# ABOUT PREFACING

Hello, welcome!

Prefaces are not for us, they are a waste of time and just make us bored and sleepy, I know it. But they are useful to tell us, you and me, something relevant.

I am not aware of your own dreams yet, but I am guessing they could be about getting a little peace, serenity, happiness and the real possibility of aiming for desires and goals. Is it right?

If you have come across these pages, you are probably the kind of person constantly trying to explain who you are, indulging about who you are, justifying who you are and everything you do. You could be that kind of person who is extremely attentive (and sensitive) to other people's judgment, perpetually on the lookout for other people's appraisals and who always has good excuses and conciliatory phrases on hand for every occasion. To be ready and respond to looks, questions, insinuations. You always control the opinion of the Others.

*The others who? Everyone else.*
From passersby throwing you unexpected glances to your parents, your friends, relatives who would like you to be different from what you are, to people on the internet from whom you feel judged. Everyone wants something from you, and that makes you nervous.

How often are others thinking the same way you are thinking? Almost never. As a matter of fact.

Your superhuman, never-ending effort is this: explaining yourself all the time. Explaining that it is not like that, that it didn't go that way, that they didn't understand, that when you said 'A' you meant 'A' and not 'B', that that day wasn't a good day, that you are different from how it looks. And you can't! You don't have the strength, the time, the way. You can't control everything. And you are exhausted. Why do you do that?

This question, I know, you have already asked yourself. At night, when you are sick, your heart bleeds and you feel like a boulder is on your chest. During the day, at work, at school, when you think the problem is that others don't understand, on the phone with your mom, with your dad, when you are holding back the tears of anger and frustration that threaten to escape and roll down your face.
Can you give yourself an answer? This one maybe: "Because it annoys me that they think something is wrong about me." That is not an answer. It is like saying "because I like it" to someone who may ask you why you like pasta.

What if we replaced *annoyance* with *Fear*? I think that would be a definition closer to reality. What if we use the word *bad* instead of the word *wrong*?

"Because I'm afraid they are going to think something bad about me."

Much better now. Fear and bad are the same words and That is exactly what we are talking about. You are afraid that others think badly of you and therefore you feel it is your duty to constantly tell them what your ideas are and because what they say is not true, you really

feel you can explain to them how things are. You constantly tell your truth. You believe that it is your call of duty, something that you can accomplish and that depends on you and nobody else.

# IT IS NOT YOUR DUTY

It is not your duty. You can't do this. It is not up to you.

*You are not doomed to be defeated; you are just fighting the wrong war.*

You are a soldier who has unnecessarily entrenched himself on the front line. It's not others who don't understand, it is you resulting from so many different things together, up to things that others see but you cannot. Listen here: you are sitting at dinner, the friend in front of you tells you you have something in the corner of your mouth, then you, in great embarrassment, run to the bathroom to remove it but, when in front of the mirror, you try to remove it from the mirror instead of from your face. Obviously, you cannot do it and blame your friend for pointing out something that is not up to you, that insensitive, right? You cannot make it, because others will never change their minds just because you tell them endlessly who you really are.

*It is not up to you because your life is not that Others', Others' opinions are not yours, Others' ideas do not belong to you and your choices do not need to be approved by anyone.*

Every time you try to convince someone, you are not actually having a real conversation, you are not listening to and you are not being listened to; you are getting hurt, you are trying to survive the pain, *you are just trying to exist*. You feel like you cannot do that if someone else says you differ from what you feel you are. But in doing so, you are giving others the proof of your existence, and you seek the Others' judgment to confirm who you are. It is absurd, isn't it?

# YOU DON'T HAVE TO PROVE ANYTHING TO ANYONE

You will not have to do it by getting a haircut, losing three or thirty kilos, or getting married, giving birth to a child or stop to be one, or by making more money. Whatever others say or do not say and think about you, you must stop hurting yourself. And only you can make it possible. How? We will try to see it together in the next few pages, if you want to follow me on this journey. One last thing before we start, if you think you are here because you have a problem, if you think you need to read these pages because you are fragile, if you feel ashamed because you cannot get by on your own, know that you are only here because you are a brave person, much more than you can imagine **and to hell with what others say.**

# ABOUT WARNING

This is not a book of Magic.

These pages contain no spells, magic formulas, or witchcraft tricks. Should I have been a Magician, I would probably be around selling potions, turning water into champagne and whatever of this kind. As a matter of fact, I would not have tried my hand in writing a book (or if I were really magical, I would have written *Harry Potter* and not this *Easy Book to Happiness*).

Reading it will not change your life in a blink of an eye, you will not be going to sleep with this book to read waking up the morning a different person, you will not instantly become more self-confident or happier, extroverted, serene, rich, debonair.

I told you, but to make it surer and clearer, I will repeat myself. I am not a witch (although I have always felt that my application to Hogwarts got lost somehow somewhere).

### Change means losing

Losing yourself, your beliefs, your comforts, losing everything you have had and you own (or you believe you own) because you face so many obstacles and walls around yourself but these walls have kept you safe; in a place may be constricting but safe.

**And losing everything is a choice.**

*A choice I can't make for you, as much as I would like to.*

You must no longer believe that you can or should entrust your life to Others, neither will you have to rely on my words uniquely.
We will look at the Reality, yes we will, and we will do it together from a new, different perspective.

This book, you are reading it today, you are reading it Now because you feel it is The Moment to Change.

Changing will be up to you, though.
With all that it involves.

*I want to get rid of unnecessary complications.*
*I want to stop worrying about everything, for everyone.*
*I want to stop feeling Guilty.*
*I want to stop sabotaging myself.*
*I want to get richer, more self-focused, happier.*
*Is that what you want?*

**Then, *my friend*, you are in the right place.**

Let us look at an example, *shall we?*
Let's say you want to be a bookseller or a bartender. I know, it is two random jobs, but give me a moment to explain. Let's say you want to become a bookseller: the chances of becoming a bookseller would increase exponentially if you entered a bookstore and asked if they were looking for staff; the chances of becoming a bartender, too, would certainly multiply if I walked into a bar to ask if they needed someone like you, with as much or as little experience as you have. You, I swear, you know what you want. You don't think so, I know.

But you know you do.

<u>When you tell yourself «you don't know it», it is because you don't trust yourself.</u>

Chains keep you tied to the ground, chains made of self-doubt. Yours. Now you have to figure out how to get rid of them all (the ones that don't let you into our notorious bar-bookshop) and proceed. *It is just a matter of asking, after all.* I know, I hear you: "But I don't know if I want to be a bookseller..." And I also hear, "What if I don't succeed? What if it is not my way? If I come to discover or understand that my vocation was another? That I could have been happier with another job, with another person?"

Exactly.
The Uncertain.
The Fear.
The Inadequacy.

You don't want to feel how you feel now, you don't want to be anymore or any longer in the situation you are in, you don't want someone to tell you what to do or feeling like you were wasting your time, your life, you don't like the job you got or the school you attend or the people you meet. You don't want what you have.

You consider two possibilities; you evaluate and imagine what might be happening in the first case, then you analyse the second opportunity and in the end, you don't know what to choose and so on, for every crossroad in life. Right? Left? Will I stop? You tell yourself how it is not easy to take your time, sit down and analyse what you really want.

Is it much easier to find any excuse to hide behind? Isn't it?

# A GOOD IDEA TO GET WHAT ONE WANTS IS TO KNOW WHAT ONE WANTS.

Too many responsibilities, too many chances to make mistakes, Fear of the judgment of others, people you don't want to disappoint, things to do. All things that almost keep you from breathing. But we are here for this: to learn how to breathe, through success, goals, joy, burdens, pain, guilt, destiny.

*There will come a time in this book* when I ask you to say goodbye to a person; when that moment comes, you will know that things will really change. Please follow me with confidence until that special moment and you will decide then whether to go ahead or not. If you do, I can teach you to understand, to accept, to achieve what you want, forever.

Without any Fear.

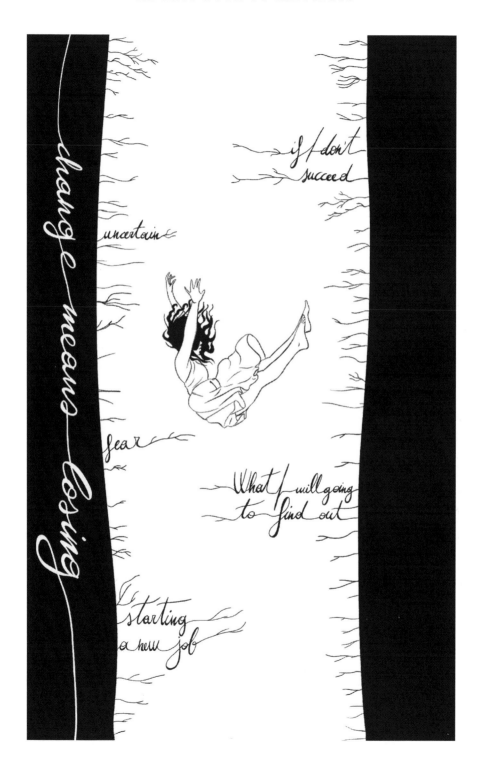

# ABOUT INTRODUCTION:
# HI THERE, I AM MARIA BEATRICE!

I am glad you have come here, thank you! After a necessary premise we have come to the most awkward and amusing part of this whole book: presentations.
Obviously, because before embarking on a journey - notwithstanding purely metaphorical as in our case - it is always better to get to know one's fellow adventurer. Even more so if this has to be one's guide.

Hello, such a pleasure to meet you!
I'm Maria Beatrice and when someone calls me Maria, I always think they are not talking to me. But many do that... Thence I, to overcome the *impasse*, the first thing I say is "You can call me Bea!" Hello! I am Bea, and I am really happy to meet you. In life, I have taken care of how things work. Through and through, as you can tell. When I was four years old, I programmed with the computer and acting at the same time. Then I went through the usual things: an academic career, a degree, a job, entrepreneurship, and we get to when you are reading this book.

Today, one of my main occupations is to help people find how to cope with their Fears and to achieve their goals. I do this in so many ways: as a consultant, as a coach, creating strategies and so on. There are many ways to do this. Thence I analyse, I study, I try to understand, I empathise, I concentrate and I try to have what it is called a *vision*.

A technical term with nothing to do with falling into a trance, seeing things that don't exist, talking to spirits, connecting with the other world and things like that. What I see belongs to reality, the most real possible reality; the *one to be built*, but that is already existing in front of me. A reality still hidden or just behind in the horizon, stripped of the burdens of judgement or self-judgement, cluttered up with paranoia, Fear, criticalities, resistances.

*The way things should be.*

The heart of the business I am analysing, the essence of the person (or company or project) that I have in front of me. I will give you an image: the sea. You look at it, you see the rocking of the waves, you listen to it, then the perspective is crunched on the horizon: the sea is there, you catch it as a whole and you think *I understand the sea*. Lucky you. But why is it so important to understand? What is it for? It is about the strategy to develop. When I do my job and I have in front of me someone who wants to understand how to achieve what he wants in life and work, someone who wants to achieve certain goals, it is of paramount importance that I can see the horizon: it is fundamental to have a vision of where you can really get to.

*And There is no limit on the horizon.*

When I picture the destination, I can drive during the journey. **I know where to go.** That is the strategy. And there is never one equal to another. It could be a marketing strategy: place a brand or product, sell it. Sometimes it is an exit strategy. To get you out of the stalemate that your own thoughts create for you.

14

Sometimes it is an awareness strategy. To measure who you are, regardless of all the rumours, regardless of the terror you have of making mistakes or making a mistake again or a dreadful future you are sure will happen. And since my consultations take place *ad personam*, I wanted a way to reach a lot more people and try to help out, in my own small way, a lot more people.

*That is why I am writing this book.*

It can be said that from the age of 4 onwards, I have never chosen which side to stand on (whether it be from a technological standpoint or from an artistic one) and have always followed both sides. Sometimes I also combine these two aspects of my career and of my journey.

Was it hard?
Not as much as it was painful.

Why painful?
Because I found myself disappointing (or believing I was) a lot of people.
And facing other people's expectations is much harder than facing yourself, isn't it?

Thence let's start, so that I can tell you how to stop feeling like you were in a motor press, in a room where all the walls of your and others' judgment are closing towards you and you feel like you were suffocating.
It is just you and me, now I will stop the motor press and we will get started.

# YESTERDAY AND TOMORROW: DO THE FUTURE AND THE PAST EXIST?

Let's start with a simple topic: past and future.

Two concepts that are part of our first achievements, as children, we learn that the past is what had happened already, and the future is what will happen. These are two conditions of time and space that we learn from the start. All pretty simple.

Past and future do exist, one was until a moment ago (and changed us) and one comes immediately after the present moment and, in the same way, it conditions us when we have to face choices. Without a hint of a doubt, right?

Bad belief and, more than that, false.

_Past and future do not exist._

Of course, you have a past, and no one doubts you have plans for the future, like everyone else.

You are right, it is true.

But if you thought about it better, you would notice how what you consider "past", the huge amount of experiences that brought you here, are only your memories.

17

Let's try to think together whether having memories and designing choices is enough to make the past and the future *exist*.
If you think about the past, what immediately comes to mind is the incredible amount of experiences, everything you have been through, everything that has led you to be the person you are today
But you don't see all those things in front of you any longer, you just have memories.

*Remembrance and nothing else, right?*

<u>*These memories, however, are not your past.*</u>

And it is because, think about it, until you bring back your memories, they don't even exist. The past is the set of your memories that exist only when you bring them, in a certain way, *back to life*.

Let me explain better, let's do this way:
if I write the word *apple* you will probably immediately think of an apple.

*An image, more or less defined, of an apple will form in your mind.*

*But what kind of apple are you going to think of?*

This image will form by combining hundreds of apples you have seen, both in person, in photos, and, maybe, painted.
Your apple combines all the apples in your memory, whatever the shape they have ever had.

**That apple is not an apple, but it is a lot of apples**: the result of your memories.

Thence let us think about two aspects.

First, before I wrote the word *apple*, were you thinking of an apple? I don't think so.
But then does that apple, the apple you imagined, exist or not?
*No. And has it ever existed?*

Maybe, in some form and somewhere, but it certainly will not be the same as the one you have imagined.

Even if I had, by pure chance, eaten an apple just before I started reading this chapter, it is impossible to think of imagining **exactly** that apple, just that, in its totality and in its entirety.

**It will remain just the image of an apple; nothing else than the mixed reflection of many apples.**

Because in your mind and memory there isn't THE APPLE, there cannot be, for example, at the same time, a view from every angle, which includes peel, pulp and seeds, colour, smell and taste.

All you have is the set of thousands of apples you have interacted with up today. And that is the way it works for everything.

We could have tried with any other word: *sea, home, chair, pain, embrace, dad* and any other tangible object or emotion, that exists, that you have touched, eaten, listened to, felt.

Because that is the way your memory, your mind, and your recollections work; a partial vision is never the same as what we consider reality.

If you were now trying to imagine an apple again, you would see the same apple, you would taste the same taste, you would perceive the same smell as an apple eaten who knows when.

If you try again tomorrow, the day after, in a week, in a month, in a year's time, you'd see a different apple.

Because that is the way it works: everything changes according to the day, the hour, the exact second you draw it from your memories.

_The past does not exist, except in our memory and memories are the only form of the past we can consider real._

Memories recall in the present something that is no longer here and is no longer now. Not in its original form, but it lives, it lives again, in one's heart as a direct, concrete experience.

 **Thus, one becomes a victim of nostalgia**, when memories fill the heart completely, without leaving any room for the present.

That apple doesn't really exist.
That apple is only the result of your knowledge filtered through your experience.

_But... What if that apple had really existed?_

I don't want to question your ability to dig back into the past. Maybe the apple you imagined is exactly the same as the apple that existed until a few days, months or years ago.

What now?

Most likely, that apple was eaten. You may have eaten it. Maybe you forgot it in the fridge or fell out of the tree and stayed in the dry leaves. If it wasn't eaten, it became dust, in any case it turned into something else and it is no longer that apple.

If I asked you to think about the apple, you would see it. For you, it would be only that apple, just as you knew it, not the rotten, not the chewed apple. You see it for what it was before all this, **for you** it still **exists.**

*But where is it?* **In the past,** *that apple is there.*

Then we can define the past as <u>**a place where all things remain motionless**</u>, frozen images of a moment, a state or a condition that no longer exists.
That can no longer exist, that has changed, mutated, precisely because it is *Past.*

**And remember, you can give to this past whatever the value you**  **want.**

That apple may be the best you have ever eaten, the worst ever, one amongst many.

That apple can be whatever apple you want. Incredible, isn't?

# REMEMBER: FROM THE LATIN RECORDARI (FROM COR, CORDIS): BRING BACK TO THE HEART

And then, if this famous apple does not exist, or simply no longer exists, even your experiences do not exist, or no longer exist. They have been there, they have trained you, but they are no longer with you. Not right now.

They come back to life only the moment you think of them:

*If you think of them, they exist, if you don't think of them, they don't exist anymore.*

Thinking of them allows them to return to the present, **to think about them gives them incredible strength.**
*You are giving them this strength.*

Memories, however, have hidden inside wounds, disappointment and failures.

And so, you come to believe that, if you have suffered or failed in the past, in the present you will not be able to live as you should. That mistake that changed you, that mistake that hurt you, that person you are not anymore, who you should be... Right? How much power can the past have?

To the question "Does the apple exist?" you would have answered in a second with a convinced, "Of course it does!" And you had to be wrong. Think about, thence, how your mind can affect your desires, your dreams, your goals. What a false connotation the mind can give them. To all memories. To all the past.

*Past doesn't exist. It doesn't exist anymore.*

Let's skip forward. Let's leave the realm of Past to reach the domain of things that still have to happen. Like the Christmas' Ghosts of Dickens' *A Christmas Carol* (my favourite is the Muppets version), but in this story, we will call in on them and not the other way round. I need not ask you the same question about the future, do I? You already know what I will tell you.

*Future doesn't exist.*

I feel you are not accepting the idea: I know, we were born and raised with stable concepts to build our lives through. It would seem like a suicide to give up two certainties such solid as past and future. But I promise you that one needs to question everything in order to change one's point of view. We have already demonstrated that Past does not exist, we will now show that the future *does not really feel right* and we will have taken a good step towards freeing you from unnecessary, tiring and painful burden. You say the future exists because you know that tomorrow you will work, that you will have to go shopping, it will rain, it will be Sunday, right?

I'm sorry I am disappointing you, but no matter how sensitive, intelligent, prepared, and attentive you may be, **you'll never really know what's going to happen until Future becomes Present and things actually happen.**

You are going to work, but you might be late, your boss might give you an unexpected day off, you might get a promotion. The salad you had planned to buy at the greengrocer might not be there. The sun might take over the sky, and bye-bye rain. It will be Sunday, but you might not spend it on the sofa and you will have a sudden desire to go jogging: after all it was supposed to rain, and instead look at that sun! If an event has occurred in the past there is no certainty that this will occur again. We are talking about your life **NOT** about a scientific experiment. We can play with probabilities and statistics, analyse every condition, say that if nothing has changed, it is likely that something that has already happened will repeat itself. But one is never sure.

<u>*Yours are assumptions, not truth.*</u>

If talking about Future, we are not drawing from the truth, but from the basket of fantasy, why do we allow this context to influence so much to leave us blocked, paralyzed?

*We are so afraid of a simple fantasy.*

I know it is not easy at all, but this is the first and most important step. You have to change your perspective on things, look at them for what they really are and give them the right name.

*Not Past, but Memory.*
*Not Future, but Fantasy.*

In this way, things are getting a little bit less scary, aren't they? Accepting that Past and Future do not exist could upset your life but for better or worse? If Past does not exist, there is no point in allowing

24

mere partial, vulnerable, changeable memories to hurt us and ruin our Present. Right?

If Future doesn't exist, we shouldn't fear a fantasy anymore, which is as likely as unlikely to come true. Right?

**<u>Having already lived an experience or a situation does not make it real again.</u>**

Now, how to live Present profiting of this renewed push is up to us to understand. Thence, let's continue in the next chapter in order to find out together what prevents us from fully living the present. Shall we go?

# ABOUT THE JOURNEY

Standing still won't help you. Close your eyes, breathe and take the first step. Walk, one step at a time, but don't stop. Whatever will happen.

Every time you say, "I can't do this," you are nurturing your Fear. Fear feeds Guilt. Guilt controls you. And if you lose control, you are not alive anymore. You have already found a thousand excuses to not move. You have assured yourself that you do not yet have everything you need to get started, that you will do it as soon as you can, that you have to get the basics first, that you have not studied enough, that you do not have the money yet, that it is not the right place, that you do not have time enough now and that it would be too tiring.

But you don't realize that the most exhausting road is just that one you have taken. A road that goes nowhere, that goes back to where it started, walking on which equals to being still. This is the path for who is pandering to Fear, for who go back to bed, once again defeated, because they could not step that first centimetre.

*Let us imagine that in front of you there is just a metre, not a thousand.*

That is the distance between you and the life you want, between you and the person you want to be. Only a metre separates you from your

27

desires, from the job of your dreams... from all your dreams! From achieving everything. And believe me, this metre will be hard, oh if it is, and tiring, and fatiguing. No one will ever say it will be easy, I will not say that.

*Because to get everything you want, you need to exploit everything you have.*

This is the only way in the world: getting something by investing every resource, 100% of yourself, with no discounts of any kind. There are no special offers on success. No Black Friday, no 3x2, no membership discount. Nothing. Just you, your life, your dreams and your commitment. This is to achieve success.

And you know what success is? Be nice. Be happy. It is not true that you don't know what you want, it is not true that you don't have what you need, you don't have enough luck. It is not true that it is not the right time, it is not true that you don't have time, it is not true that it is too tiring. The only limit between you and the second centimetre is your Fear. And you can defeat it. Your Fear right now is you.

**Your only limitation is yourself.**

Disguised as judgment, disguised as wisdom, disguised as insecurity, disguised as knowledge, disguised as reflection. You put your emotions in front of you, you let them guide you, but you are not just what you feel. The voice that whispers to you it would be safer to wait a little longer, the one that repeats to you "Be careful, be careful", the one that indicates one by one all the things that could also go wrong. Those voices aren't your voice.

You are scared, but it is just a moment, *this very moment*, but you don't know what it will be like soon after, and That is why you can't stop. You don't know if the water will be really cold, if you pass the next curve the road will be deserted. You don't know and you can't hold yourself back. Jump or walk, whatever your way is. Begin. There is nothing else you have to do today: start. You have already travelled the first centimetre, without even realizing it, and nothing and no one will stop you. The centimetre will become a metre and metres and you will get to where you wanted.

One step at a time, breathing, looking at the sky in front of you and the horizon. Do it, every day, walk, follow the road to be happy. I will be there to tell you this "Don't you see it? There was not so much to be changed within you, but so much to take care of: your wounds". All you have to do is walking. Keep walking, again and again.

*But to get where?* You ask me.

Walking is a movement and if you start your motion it is just to get somewhere, right? Walking is another way to tell yourself and others you are going somewhere. Everything that has passed, each recollection of yours, every tear or wound, everything has shaped you into the person you are.

# TO STOP FEELING WRONG, YOU DON'T HAVE TO CHANGE, YOU HAVE TO WALK.

All you have experienced is woven into the fibres of your being, like patches on a dress that everyday changes, mutates and transforms. Every choice made, every sea sailed, every step taken in every direction. All this is on your body, in your mind, you could see them and touch them hadn't they mixed, fused and melted. And, despite that, you still want to get there. You don't want the travel, you don't want the discovery, you don't want the happiness. You just want to get to that goal, as if the destination would change everything.

Reach the money or get the person who will make you happy, the job you dream, the right friends, the right clothes, the right house. To reach the goal to fill what you feel is missing just filling the emptiness with salted water. You are tired because walking has always meant going full speed, for everyone and for everything. To do so, you pulled the rope, tried running through the pain and your knees gave way. That is why you stopped.

Tired of not being seen or heard.
Tired of never being considered a man.
Tired of not being taken into account.
Tired of giving everything you have.

That is why you want to get there, because you feel like you have never gotten anywhere. Because if they abandoned you, if they fired you, if they betrayed you, if they hurt you, if they let you down, if they treated you badly, looked down on you, if they took you for granted, so often, for a lifetime, then it means you arrived nowhere. *You think that, but you are wrong.*

*You want to arrive, but you should just leave.*

*You are already there*, even if you haven't seen the arrival signs. Because you only get there to leave again. There is no point to reach, no definitive goal, no line to be crossed. Walking is not a where, but a why. You have to leave, get back on the road, keep walking. Whatever happens. But how? With no idea where you are going, what you will do and how you will do it.

But why? Because your hands will withstand the force of the wind pulling the ropes of your sails. Leave and feel lost, feel uncomfortable. Be afraid, live it, face it. Because **it is not real courage if you are not afraid** and no journey that was ever been worth it had good planning.

Your life, that is the most unique experience in the world. Unmatchable. Unrepeatable. No one will ever be able to live this very journey instead of yours. Then leave, go. Without wondering where you want to get to but go wherever your boat at least stays afloat. Face the sea, overcome the storm, watch your boat withstand any impact. Because then you will know, the sea of uncertainty around you, that you have chosen.

# GO ANYWHERE YOUR BOAT STAYS AFLOAT.

# ABOUT EMOTIONS

You know those days when you haven't even opened your eyes yet and you already know that it will be a bad day? It doesn't matter what day of the week it is. If it is a day off, the problem will be wasting time. If it is a working day the problem will be making a mistake in front of everyone. Being able to rest, or having to rest, gives you anxiety (such an ugly and uncomfortable word). Wasting time? Never. At work you must deal with others, no matter if you like it or not. You still must have your breakfast.

The head is already quite full of worries, there is no room for anything else. You already know that confrontation with someone else will come sooner or later: and you will have to answer questions like these:
"But why are you always complaining?" or "Why are you always answering so nastily?"

Leave alone everyone's favourite statement: "Come on, it is nothing, it will pass!"
Because, usually, everything that happens to others is a *disaster* and what happens to you is *nothing*. Right?

And although according to everyone, it is *nothing*, your anxiety doesn't go away, you are still there and the only idea of disappointing someone is still heavier than disappointing yourself.

This is one of those days that just being alive, breathing or getting out of bed, is a heroic act. Heroism that no one can see. Not having burst into tears in front of the salesman is an unparalleled gesture of courage.

*You are a hero, even if no one knows.*

Today is a horrendous day and you still think you are a horrible person. *An obsessive thought that does not leave your mind.*

Please, note: you are here, you are still here, today is a horrendous day, you have got any reason, but it must be okay. Today is a horrible day, but you are not this day.

*It is by no means necessary to judge ourselves in this way.*

It is just a bad day. A bad week. A bad month. A bad year. The next five years may be, but that would not make you a bad or wrong person, it doesn't define you likewise.

*A wrong day can't define you as a wrong person.*

*Things can go wrong until they will be okay. And it will be just on you if and when things will go right.*

*As, believe me, things will get better.*

34

If you are sad or angry, your mood is at its bluest, you are red with shame, your legs are shaking for Fear, you are neither crazy nor coward.

You are just someone who is sad, angry, ashamed, who is afraid. **You are not sadness. Neither anger nor Fear. Not even shame.**

## Your emotions don't define you at all.

If you are crying, you are not weak, if you are sad, you are not depressed, if you are angry, you are not violent and so on. Leave it to your emotions to express what you feel, do not use them to define yourself and don't let others do it. They are useful words to understand each other, but they do not define a character. They do not define the complex variable identity of a human being. You can't enclose a personality inside a word. You can't homologate something such multifaceted as emotions.

### *You should not think that emotions are the person who feels them.*

Why is this happening? Because for convenience, we needed to catalogue things. We need to name them, categorize them, to make ourselves understood, and the more the world becomes big and international the more we need models. And then we can say, without being greedy that in this world we should all be more or less happy, slim, rich and beautiful (Quoting the famous 1960s socialite Gloria Guinness, amongst Truman Capote's "Fifth Avenue's Swans" and best friends, «One can't be ever too rich or to slim»). If ugly at least clever. Stupid and rude. And so on. You may finish to believe it, you end up convincing yourself this is reality and then you ask yourself: *why*

*am I not like that? Why am I so sad? I shouldn't be sad. Why am I al-
ways angry? I shouldn't be angry.*

# YOU ARE NOT YOUR EMOTIONS.

Two, three, four or five times a day, you think that exhaustion has
now gripped you in its arms and will never let you go, don't you?
That you are too tired not to be sad or angry. Fatigue is the blanket
you always keep with you, that you drag around the house and even
wear to work, when you go shopping or go out with friends for a beer
or a bottle of wine (drinking the whole bottle by yourself). Tiredness
hides every feeling, all the different emotions, sensations, nuances
you would have the right to feel and instead, you no longer feel. Just
tiredness, a single name that collects everything thence farewell to
everything you should experience and to which you should give a
name.

You may also drown in tiredness because you have swallowed too
many emotions and all at once. Emotional greed, you have had too
much, and now you are nauseated. Nothing other than sitting at the
table at lunch, swallowing without even chewing, making the meal
tasteless, heavy. It will be difficult to find the strength to dine, fatigue
will be the master: an emotional fatigue? Physical?

The same happens after you bottle emotion after emotion, almost
automatically, without even realizing that you have experienced
them. Emotions that fill our backpack and make us slower and heavier every day. We have lost enthusiasm, and sensations, instead of giv-

ing us excitement, make us tired. Emotions no longer have colour, you don't distinguish them anymore, you don't give yourself time to feel who they are, what they are, how you react or you might react to them and, above all: how they make you feel if you give them way.

*It is not tiredness: it is anguish.*

You don't want to feel these emotions. Do everything you can to leave them where they are, to push them away, to push them back in, to distract you while you feel them, you don't want to face them.

*You will not allow yourself to face them.*

Do you remember the aforementioned blanket? What is a blanket doing? Covers, precisely. Its mantle hides everything, you do not even know what the word tired really means because you replace it with Fear, terror, pain, worry, shame, humiliation. But also, joy, success, love, excitement, sexuality. Everything.

*Fatigue is not an emotion.*

Fatigue should not become a substitute meal for emotions. The beverage big enough to survive for a day, to sleep but not to dream. Fatigue is not an escape. Tiredness doesn't help you live. You have to look at how you feel. You have to listen to how you feel. You have to put yourself in your shoes even if it hurts, even if it is scary. Know who you are, know what you feel. How? Listening to yourself. Looking under the blanket. Why are you tired? Is it Fear? Well, let's call it Fear. Is it shame because you failed? Well, call it shame. That is all you have to do now. Just give it a name.

Try it. Try to replace fatigue with your real emotion. Strive to go beyond the surface, look at the nuances. Emotions are not something static, they are not all the same and cannot be represented in the same way for everyone, they are not emoticons, smiley faces, stickers, emojis. And again: when you say you are angry, do you try to think what all those things, situations, people that make you angry have in common? You are the common denominator, but there will also be something else. Have a little patience, everything will become clearer. Quietly.

**That doesn't mean being slow**, because slowness is another one of those things that doesn't exist. I will tell you one thing in advance: you can't try to solve your feelings with a trick. You can't hope to stop being the way you are, but you can work to understand it. At your pace. And that means really trying to change, bit by bit, to be happy and live your emotions, whatever they may be.

If you follow my advice these days, at some point, you may feel overwhelmed by all those emotions that you have been hiding for who knows how long (since forever?). There could be many and conflicting. Don't be scared, you are moving forward in the right direction.

You don't know it, but you are fighting an enemy: the Unconscious.

*Who is it? What is it doing?*

*Basically, it keeps you alive.*

It doesn't take your well-being into consideration because it doesn't know what that means. It grew up with you from the first few minutes of life and knows everything about you, but it doesn't fit unless you teach it.

Unconscious is harsh

It is harsh about making you react to things always the same way because that is how it knows you will stand on your feet. In principle, Unconscious organizes and monitors all that is ordinary, not dangerous and common. Things it can handle without having to disturb us. A kind of autopilot that when the road is clear, without traffic or curves, proceeds towards home, but when it recognizes an obstacle, it wakes us up, inviting us to take back control and act. The concept of danger and risk determines its behaviour, the settings of the autopilot. It reacts to the things that happen by making us feel certain emotions or not, sometimes to protect us: it is the unconscious that puts into operation a defence mechanism, which pushes us to survive without suffering beyond our possibilities, without putting ourselves in crisis beyond our capacity for endurance. But who told the unconscious that A is dangerous and B is not? Our experiences, our very first ones, our parents, their presence or absence, what we have seen, what we have learned in our context, at school, at home. I mean ourselves.

*You.*

We are the ones who defined the *settings*, we have taught Unconscious what is dangerous, what we must defend ourselves from. **Without knowing it**, of course. If only Unconscious could be taught in kindergarten.

*Today the unconscious may be fighting enemies not even any longer existing.*

The darkness, the fear that your parents will leave, will divorce, the need to see a certain image in the mirror otherwise people will not love you, the will to achieve perfection because only then others will believe that they need you and you will never be left alone.

*These are all defences, all roads, all mechanisms of the unconscious.*

They keep you alive but the stiffer they become, the more they are the only resort you have to face the life events, the more stuck you feel.

We may have had experiences that conditioned us to such an extent that we were forced to set our unconscious into an overly defensive mode. To live in a whole new way, to free ourselves from the unconscious control of the Unconscious – forgive the pun - we need to change ourselves. To give it new signals, to give it new directions to choose from: we have to loosen the grip. You have to change yourself and doing it is the hardest thing in the world, I know, but you can. You have to dig, while listening, to investigate the reasons for your action and once you reach them, move them. Like boulders obstructing the road. You have to move them and free new paths. You will find all the characteristics that form your personality, your certainties, what you call ethics, values. All things with nothing to do with moral choices but are fully subjugated to the unconscious.

The Guilt, for instance; the yardstick for the goodness of our actions, what represents us and corresponds to what we are, what we want and what we will do.

*A small anticipation: Guilt is a scam. A no-exit cage that keeps us in the very where we want ourselves to stay (but a whole chapter will be dedicated to the subject).*

You have to change. You keep repeating it. You know it and you are convinced because you can no longer feel how you feel, but you face the Fear of having to abandon your certainties. So much, too much Fear and it becomes the reason you never change. You can't leave your tracks; you are not able to abandon the route because you should give up that **blind belief** of **needing** to foresee every turn of the road before proceeding.

Like it was possible!!!
**It isn't.**
Let's read this sentence again.

*Blind conviction*
Blind, indeed
*It is not a random choice, actually.*

I chose this adjective because that belief is nothing real, blind in this case means no way out (such as corners or alleys). It is again another defence of Unconscious to protect you, itself and the existing order of things. If you change, when you change, everything is turned upside down; it is a small moment of chaos to reach a new order, but your Unconscious doesn't perceive it in this way and only notices the danger. Changing means getting to the side of the road and crossing it.

*It means wading through the river.*
*It means taking the one step up.*

But the Unconscious sees only the cars passing by and doesn't see the other side of the sidewalks. The Unconscious observes only the surface of the water, crisped by the wind, but not the green lawn at the other side. The unconscious only notices the gap between each step and another and doesn't consider that the higher you climb, the happier you feel. Fear, the defence of the defences, blocks you and paralyzes you. Feeling it when you are about to change is normal, but it doesn't have to stop you.

*Promise me you will not stop.*

The unconscious is an alert light you can ignore. If you are afraid it will never happen, it will never happen. If you think you will never wake up happy, feeling like you are what you wanted to be, you will never wake up that way. If you don't think you could live without taking on you others' responsibilities (because that is the only way you think others will love you) and not feeling guilty, well: you'll never live and always feel like an impostor.

Do you know why you feel like an impostor?
Because when you do something, you don't do it for someone else. **You do it for yourself, for your Unconscious.** You don't buy just for the sake of buying. You don't cook just for cooking. Don't drink for fun. You don't eat to feed. You are not on a diet because it will do you good. You don't live just to live. You do it because you have to prove to something inside you it is worth it. That you are good, right, strong, capable, incorruptible. And when the others point out some flaws, a few twists in your dress, you feel like an impostor. Because you didn't do that for the reason you proclaim, in all honesty.

You did it so you wouldn't get sick. Better; to be less sick. To lower the anguish, the anxiety, the Guilt. Here is the Deception.

*Here is the Impostor.*

Now listen to me: if you believe that it is over and it will be nothing like before, that you will not survive this pain, that you will not make it through, *just look back at your yesterday*. Look at your memory of yesterday and don't be fooled by the Unconscious.

# YOUR UNCONSCIOUS CONSTANTLY DEMANDS YOU TO BE VALIDATED AND YOU ALLOW IT, ALL THE TIME.

Yesterday was the same darkness. You were just as afraid you would not make it. And yet look, think about it: it is today, another day and you are still here. You thought nothing would change. Everything you learned and believed would be helpful, the point you established as arrival, the goal you so longed for. *Nothing is real.* This make-believe caught you up and now it will not let you go. This image is a world you built in your mind stick after stick, to create Something above you that would confirm you as capable. Skillful. Smart. As if you need a goal to feel fulfilled, as if it was never enough what you did today. Tomorrow will always be the day of your happiness. *Always tomorrow.* A Mecca to be reached and in which to say, finally and without a doubt, "Yes, I did it". Shout it at yourself and others, shut them up in the face of your undeniable victory. But look at that goal: it never seems closer, not even by one step, does it? You feel tired because you feel like you are walking in the desert and never reaching the horizon, surrounded by dunes which are always the same and not even the hint of an oasis. Not even the mirage of a sip of water. Just storms, sand and sun. Because there will always be something that will prevent you from reaching it until you understand that you are the one pushing away the love you are longing for.

*You are the one who pushes your goal away one step at a time.*

Every time you get up in the morning, you move your happiness one day forward, you are like a crazy clock that insists on always showing an extra hour. And you did it all by yourself, you are the hand that turns the hands of the clock.

*Feeling you are not worth enough. That the person you are with is not worth enough. That your children or parents or employers or colleagues or friends or partners are not worth enough.*

There is a whole world inside of you that you haven't even seen yet and you just close your eyes, take a breath and accept that for today you don't have to do anything more, that no one has to do anything more, so that you can be yourself and be accepted for exactly that person you are. Nothing is wrong with that. You are safe.

*You are not an impostor.*

 Give yourself time to experience emotions you have not lived yet. Give yourself time to experience feelings you have not tasted yet.

**Time is infinite, because past and future do not exist.**

You have all the time.

# ABOUT CONTROL

If you remember in the last chapter, I mentioned the blind belief - and I stress "blind" - that you can control everything in your life. I have already said this, but better to be clear and unequivocal: all bullshit. You control nothing, but you are under the illusion you can do it. Why? Because otherwise you would panic. You would be surprised to see how many things you do every day just to stay in control. There is no corner of the planet, place in the world, not even one, where you will find written on the wall:

*Rule number 1: Always say yes, even to what sucks.*

There are dictatorships, countries in the world where you are not free to choose what to do, where a *no* can cost your life. True, right, but you are hiding behind a hyperbole. You are not under dictatorship, There is no regime controlling you. And yet you keep saying yes to anything that makes your stomach turn upside down and yourself feeling unfit. You keep believing you are controlling things by saying yes to everything, and you don't realize you are under control instead. Why? We've seen how you are letting the unconscious drive you, now let's try together to figure out exactly how it works in real life. In real life you do it by lying:

# WHAT YOU HIDE CONTROLS YOU.

You try to lie. And you don't do it out of malice, but because sometimes it is the easiest solution. You lie to your mother, your father, your sister, your brother, your partner, and so on. You even lie to your boss. Truth brings questions and questions need justification, don't they? Justifications about your mistakes - or those you think being so. Then better a lie, another omission. But how much does each lie weigh? A thousand yourselves rebelling and screaming at that lie. A thousand yourselves who remember every moment you said another lie, until the numbness. The Fear of being discovered, caught, rumbled.

 *The Impostor Syndrome that wakes you up at night and doesn't make you sleep anymore.*

But yours are just innocent lies, nothing serious. Innocent lies, right? But this is the only life you have, the only chance to really be you. You and no one else. And you spend your life telling lies so as not to fight against others' opinion.

*Lying is not an option, it is a defence.*

Because lies control you and keep you safe. And want you to be controlled or to be free? And are you ready to get out of the protective fence of lies to be happy? Well. Then know that even always saying *yes* is not a solution. You do it to feel less inadequate, because you think you are appreciated and loved only this way and then you put in a series of yeses. A long series of yeses.

To your indulgence, to fatigue that sticks you watching another TV series, to the litres of alcohol you drink, masked under friendly names such as *aperitive* and indulgent adjectives such as *deserved*, you keep saying yes to men or women who are not for you, you let them mistreat you and then you belittle them, in an attempt of taking back your control. You say yes to your parents or your children, to people you made dictators of your life and that can use you and your time as they please. These are the yeses, it is them and your conviction. The only regime that is controlling you, You say yes to a job you hate, to your boss you cannot stand, to your colleagues you detest, but that you cannot ignore or contradict, Fearing the fact that they could have a bad opinion about you. Does it sound like familiar sentences, isn't it? We have already talked about it: you try to control reality and you end up being controlled, worried about what others might think of you. Then you find yourself in bed, looking at the ceiling and thinking:

*How could that happen and when have things started to be this way?*

Things, believe me, went this way in the exact moment you convinced yourself that you could reach a perfection that actually doesn't exist. This uneasiness began the day you thought you could make everyone happy, that you could accomplish anything, that you could always be good. But good for whom? For others, obviously. Why? Because you cannot and you don't want to ask for help. You know that they only way to please someone, to keep him alive, is to look after him yourself. 100%. *Look after= Control.* Your mother demanded it, your father demanded it, then at school and finally at work. You don't ask for help, you just have to give over and over to have others thinking of you as indispensable, that without you, they can't carry on, and that is the way you believe you keep them close.

But it doesn't work, does it?

You pursue Perfection, an excellence you believe being universal, but it is just a subjective (unfortunately), distorted vision of things: you see others and yourself, you create the right perspective to avoid a forced change and to make just *a little* sacrifice; an infinite series, but overall bearable, of *yeses*.
*And what happens when you say yes and others rebel? When they are ungrateful? When they leave you? When they don't give you a promotion, when they choose other friends and not you. What happens then?*

Where does what you call "generosity" end? A black hole of commiseration and terror in which you do not even want to enter will open. Because if you were already in the view of accepting your emotions, you would live this Fear and give it an answer: *they do not love me, and this makes me suffer. They don't love me like I would like to be loved and that makes me suffer.* And you could begin to feel free. Don't choose the wrong path again by saying that nobody deserves you, closing all the doors and just staying there, still like a piece of ice. Why? I have already told you why: because you are doing it to survive, your unconscious is doing it for you.

## To be loved

Don't let us be misunderstood; at the end of the day you are good to people, far from me saying the opposite. The point, unfortunately, is that the reason, the push, is not this, so you screw yourself over with your own hands. Cheating with your own cards and continuing to play becomes difficult. You have had the sentence "I have to make everyone love me" in your brain. Well concealed but tattooed. Phrases like *I have to be perfect, I am not enough, I don't do enough*, they should not exist anywhere in the world, leave alone in your head. It is nothing but a lie.

A big, big lie and you can stop repeating it right now! You are enough, you are all right, they will love you. They will love you the way you are, I swear.

# THEY ARE GOING TO LOVE YOU FOR WHO YOU ARE.

"Nothing is under your control" does not mean you have to resign yourself to the fatality of things, that nothing depends on you. I am not at all advising you on a life without responsibility and consequences.

**The responsibility is yours, all yours, control is not.**

You are responsible for your actions, your thoughts, your feelings, your desires, your choices, your life, but you are not in control of them.

**You can't control what happens.**

You can't control the consequences of your words. You can't control what others think. You can't control what others do, say, imagine.

## You are you and you end up with you.

I work in marketing, as I said at the beginning, and I know that manipulation can be an incredibly powerful weapon. I use it when I plan an ad campaign, I know it, but if I applied it in everyday life by using it in whichever relationship of mine, I should be unhappy. You can't imagine how much. There are techniques on techniques to convince a person: you can make them believe many things, and make them do a lot of things simply by creating an urgency. **Urgency** is the key word. If you have created the right amount of urgency you can get anyone to buy any product, giving it the illusion of a need that it does not really have. With these techniques, you can also influence a vote, creating Fears that do not exist, needs that are not real, but this illusion lasts as long as a snap of your fingers, or two.

Just like going shopping: you buy a new dress, you are happy, you come home and it is already over. What was in your head before, has materialized, you have only an empty wallet and one less place in the closet.

Imagine this:

You are in bed after a busier evening than usual, you drank. You have done things you don't like; you choose which ones: did you scream? Fight? Kiss? Did you sleep with someone? Did you talk bad about anyone? Everything matters. How are you feeling? Teased, full of shame and Guilt. Why? Because if you were in control, you'd have acted differently and if you are not in control, you feel like you are dying.

Yesterday, instead of your unconscious (which you silenced with alcohol) you let the alcohol speak for you (*It is not like It is a genius Itself*) and today your unconscious does what? It makes you feel bad. Because you, let's remember, have decided that you must please everyone and always and if you do not, no one will ever love you, you will never be worthy enough of anyone's love. Just by *doing* you will you be appreciated. Not *being but doing.* Do you feel manipulated now? By whom? By your unconscious, meaning yourself. You can't build your relationships that way. You can't build yourself. You can't get what you want. **You can't, no one can.**

"But if others..." The usual question.

Don't think about what others will decide to do anymore: **that is not at all a responsibility of yours.**

But you don't want responsibility, do you? You just want control. You just want to be able to decide for them too, so you have everything in your hands. Everything and everyone. Thence no one can hurt you, no one will ever leave you, no one will betray you, no one will disappoint you or your expectations, no one will abandon you, no one will speak ill of you and of your drunkenness yesterday.

If you just take responsibility for what you are doing without - and I must stress this, without - taking it out on everyone you think isn't doing the right thing or they haven't done the right thing or they won't do the right thing, you should be free of Guilt at last. You wouldn't try it, you wouldn't try it on someone else. Your ex-husband who deserted you, your boss, the friend who lied to you and so on.

## <u>If you get rid of Guilt, you could finally take control of your life and stop trying to control what's not up to you.</u>

But do you know why you are constantly trying to make someone feel Guilty? Because That is how they taught you. They taught you that feeling Guilty is the right feeling for an endless series of situations we could easily sum up as *you didn't do, say, think what I* wanted. When things get out of our control, when people act arbitrarily, we activate the Guilt mechanism. Why?

**Because it is the only form of control you really know, the one that works on others or at least keeps you under the illusion of a functioning person.**

But you control nothing but your life. You are only responsible for this and nothing else. *If you are happy, it is your responsibility. If you are suffering, it is your responsibility.* Have you ever thought about that?

When you understand that the only thing you can really control is only your way of responding to what happens to you every day, which you already have in your heart and mind, with all the skills to direct what surrounds you, to identify the point of arrival and the chosen path to get there, then you would be happy. When you understand that you have to act and respond to things, not manage them for Fear they will differ from how you expected them to be, how you desired them to be, how you think they should go, then you will be happy. Nothing makes you worse in the eyes of others than trying to control them and control their lives. But that is what you want, right? To put people to the test and see if they will stay. *Because you are the impostor.*

# IF SOMETHING IS LIMITING YOUR LIFE YOU CAN GO TO THERAPY (AND YOU WILL LIKE IT).

You can always go to therapy. Therapy, why not? "But how...?" you will say. "This is a book that should help me and instead tells me I have to go to therapy?" Yes, and that is how I will really help you, just in case this book should be not enough. Because there are things we can do on our own and others we cannot, and we need to understand if it is more important that you get help from someone else besides me.

If you break your knee, if you have a high fever, if you have had an accident, you go to the doctor. If you or someone else does not feel good in the middle of the night, no one would think twice before calling an ambulance. All normal. If someone is sick, you go to the doctor, nothing absurd. If you are sick because you can't sleep even after an exhausting day, because you are even afraid of your own shadow, because you are prey to the anxiety that paralyzes you, because sometimes you can't even get out of bed. If you open your eyes and think you are worth nothing. If you wonder what the point of is continuing to live. If you imagine that, at the end of the day, it makes little sense to stay here. If you drink too much, if you smoke too much, if you eat too little or just eat too much.

If you bear the marks of these excesses, if you see your body breaking under the weight, why not go to the doctor? *But it is all different,* you say. You are still hiding, once again behind a thin, transparent wall. The opinion of Others, once again. The common opinion, the shame, the embarrassment, the belief you do not need help. But if what's going on inside you limits you every day as you had been limited by a head-on collision *at 120 km/h on the highway,* you can't pretend that nothing has happened. After such an accident you go to the hospital, you rely on doctors, you undertake a path of rehabilitation because otherwise, it is impossible to continue living. And then you respond to the same logic and behave the same way.

**If what you feel inside you limits you, debilitates you, keeps you locked inside the house: <u>you have</u> to go to therapy.**

Go to the psychologist, pick a psychoanalyst. Private ones cost money, right? But you can forgo a dinner or a dress and here's the money for a session. And if there is not even this money, then you can go to your GP to access therapy via your health service: it will cost much less and it will be affordable for you. Because I don't know what you imagine and what you associate with the word *psychotherapist,* but I assure you that is exactly what it does: it removes the obstacles that have formed, that have collapsed and crashed in your way during all the years of your life. It cleans up the path and helps you get familiar with the new roads to walk, run, slide, skate, swerve, fall, roll on without having to stop because the road is blocked.

The psychotherapist puts the road surface of your life in order.

**<u>I don't want to make therapy look like a game; it is not.</u>**

**<u>Going to therapy is an act of bravery</u>**, it takes the same amount of courage for any other difficult action. You will have to fight and once you realize it is a gesture you are making for yourself, here you have to face yourself. Because the hardest part is the challenge against you. A fight One against One in which you have to put in everything you have. Because it is heavy, it empties you, it takes away your energy. But you can do it. See it as something beautiful, sexy and successful. It is not true that they will think you are weird, that you are crazy. Today, all the men and women who have achieved great feats have allowed themselves to be helped. Not because they were weak... Quite the opposite.

*You did it by buying this book, too, right?*

On the contrary, it is a matter of strength: <u>facing one's own limits and Fears makes us free</u>, let all our potential explode, without any limitations. Do yourself a big favour and do not go to therapy because "I want to improve my ability to speak in public" or "because I want to find out more about myself", you do not need to mask your request for help. You do not have to. Be honest, just be honest!
It will help you. Special people know how to get help, you are one of them.

And if what is in your head is holding you back and has not yet limited you to the point that you have to change your lifestyle habits (sleep, eat, leave the house, work, etc.) then we can move forward together, we can still do a lot.

# ABOUT OTHERS AND OURSELVES: THE GAME WE PLAY.

Life is not a game, but how much time do we spend *playing?* An infinity. And among our favourite games is that to *change*, or to suppose of changing. Indeed, even better: the change of the world, Others ' world, but never ours.

We just saw it, changing ourselves is very difficult. We have to come to terms with the most real and profound part of ourselves: we have to dig, move boulders, get closer to the roots. It is very difficult to move roots without severing them, living with the constant Fear of change. We are slaves to what we believe, of our *blind conviction,* we imagine ourselves as immutable beings, who cannot change without having to die. Phrases like *I am the kind of person who, I am a person who, I am one of those people who...* Are they familiar to you? They are the portrait, the photograph of those who imagine themselves eternally equal, unable to see themselves even a little different from how it is. To overcome this way of thinking, is a life challenge.

**Not a challenge but THE challenge.**

However, as much as we are aware that changing ourselves is extremely difficult, there is no day when we think we cannot change Others.

*There is no day that passes in which we are not **certain**, damn certain, that changing others is possible.*

We are not only convinced that we could do this, and we will try again in our most desperate attempts, but we even come to believe that changing a person is small business. Changing ourselves is difficult, we do not even try, but we spend a good part of our lives trying to change Others. Weird, isn't it? We do it every day because we are sure it is a doable operation. How to convince a child to eat vegetables, just because we are big, and we tell him every day that *vegetables are good for us.*

The biggest misconception is this: we think that changing a person is simple, so simple we do not even hypothesise a *plan b*, we do not prepare for possible emergencies, changes of course. We think that changing a person is a piece of cake, a bit like driving from home to work. Something we do every day and do not worry about much: what could go wrong? We do not prepare a sandwich for a possible gigantic traffic jam, we do not phone our loved ones to warn them of the trip, we do not check the tire pressure. *Come on, that would be ridiculous: we are just going to work.* What does it take? We do it every day.

We reason in the same way when we think we can change a person and we do it even if, in reality, we have never changed anyone. We leave for this journey without considering anything unexpected, without imagining any variation. We never consider that changing a person is impossible and we do not evaluate other alternatives. For us, the alternatives do not exist, no light bulb in the brain is turned on. Let's imagine that it is that simple, we work to do it, we consume a lot of our energy, and we fail in the end.

**We fail miserably.**

Without ever looking up to look around us, never having considered an alternative. And, above all, without having even had half a real chance of succeeding. Tolstoy said: *Everyone thinks about changing the world, but no one thinks of changing himself.*

I am saying that, too.

A phrase that tickles our minds, that almost makes us smile: because each of us knows that we have tried to change things, knows that we have put energy and effort into it but that we have achieved little or no results. And yet we still think we can change Others. How can we think that? But above all, one might ask: *why do we feel the desire to change Others?* It would seem almost an instinct, a deformation of thought. Changing others is like playing a game every day, changing them in small or big ways, in the important affairs of life or in meaningless nonsense. Always sacrificing considerable energy, let us be clear. This is a game we take very seriously, we are like restless children who all find themselves sweaty, without strength, exhausted by their favourite game: an endless game, which never ends, because we will never be able to change Others.

You don't think you are doing the same, do you? You think that changing people means revolutionising them, that you can succeed, that it is for their own good. *Bullshit.* Wanting to change people also means telling them how to dress, how to talk, what to say and what to do in any given situation by emphasising what they did wrong.

61

**Wrong in your** opinion, it is obvious.

Because if they were different, they would love you, wouldn't they? If they were different, would they understand how you are? Or even, if they were different, things would be easier, simpler, if they would only understand that what you are saying is not effective, right? Why do you insist on making mistakes? Wanting to change a person also means giving opinions that you feel *are due* when in fact, they are unsolicited, but you do not realize it: because for you, that is your truth, the eternal truth that the other person must also share, accept, apply. You defend yourself, behind the phrase "but they asked me for help" or "but what should I do, let them suffer?"

*We all do, we keep doing it.*

And we do it with our children, friends, partners, companions. With colleagues, with employees, with boyfriends, husbands, girlfriends and lovers... *my mother even does it with neighbours.*

Often in our relationships, we play to the mechanics: we choose some people, but without accepting them for who they are, ready to change them by replacing some *pieces*. We analyze the person next to us, highlight the aspects we do not like and try in every way to change them. "He is shy and I like him, but he can't stay quiet all day." "She is very smart, but she can't behave like that when we argue." "He is nice, but he can't make friends with anyone." " She is very beautiful though she can't dress like that when I'm not there." "If he just didn't call his mother a hundred times a day, it would be perfect."

*If only they didn't do it, if they just didn't say, if they just didn't think.*

And we end with *they need to be changed.* We do it with everyone, I have already said: husbands, boyfriends, companions, wives, mothers, fathers, children, priests and accountants. Let's try to change that person for the most random reasons: if we talk about someone related to us by blood (children, parents, relatives of any degree) we know that we cannot replace them and, believing that we have somehow failed in their education, we try to remedy the situation. Or we were unlucky and then we try to kick bad luck away, claiming to do it for their own good, but in fact, we only do it because we can't accept them.

*We don't want to accept them for who they are.*

If it is someone we have chosen, someone we could let go, someone obviously not for us, we do not have the courage to do so. We can't admit we made a mistake; we can't accept that we've *failed* (you always think There is a failure). We do not accept what we believe to be a mistake (instead of a simple choice), incompatibility perhaps, and try to make the person perfect for us.

We never consider - and say I <u>never</u> - the idea of accepting them for who they are. Confronting others is useful, otherwise, I wouldn't be here writing for you. But we must be able to distinguish, to consider the person in front of you and their actual capability to help. This is true in any situation, not only when there is a matter of vital importance at stake: we are social, we like to chat, discuss, listen to the opinion of Others. But we must not allow ourselves to be influenced by anything, the first sentence heard must not push us to change course. There is always our heart to reckon with.

# YOU'RE ASKING FOR INFORMATION FROM SOMEONE WHO'S NEVER BEEN WHERE YOU WANT TO GO.

Because you can't always trust Others. With this, I do not want to appear misanthropic, this is not the meaning: people cannot always be trusted not because they are bad, evil, desire our evil, our suffering or defeat but because they often tend not to be honest or useful. In what sense? Follow me in this example.

Imagine you are traveling in a city you don't know. You are out and about, you see the map, but you just don't find the destination you'd like to reach. Then stop the first person passing by. If they are a tourist, they shall probably respond by saying something like, "I'm sorry, I can't help you. I'm not from here." But is that what anyone would do? I wouldn't swear by it. Running into a second person, maybe someone born in that city, I bet they would give you some help by saying, "Go over there, turn right," but is our destination really at the next right turn? Not always. Because there is a kind of obligation that snaps into the heads of those who are questioned, a mixture of the shame of not knowing - for some ones - and the belief of knowing everything - for other ones. If you ask someone for advice in your everyday life to get something that you care about, it is very unlikely you shall be told, "I'm sorry, I have no idea how to do it," with the addition of phrases like "But I'm on your side," "I think it is a great idea" or "If you need anything else, I'm here." No, people are often like that citizen driven by who knows what instinct, who will tell you about how to reach somewhere they have never seen, never understood, never faced, never studied. They have often never even thought about it and perhaps didn't believe it existed before you talked to them about it.

I'd like to make it clear that you can't be guided by anyone. You must not blame others if they give you the wrong directions; you have to ask yourself, "Why do I care so much about having someone to guide me, someone whose opinion I don't even know if I care about, if I can trust it, if it is going to be reliable?"

I'll answer this for you: because, simply, it is not of an opinion you are looking for, but of approval. Once again, you prefer not to listen to your heart, just to hear someone tell you how interesting the trip you planned is, how brilliant the idea you had is, how funny the story you wrote is. You asked for help because you want compliments. You wait for them; *you demand* them and then maybe you are sick of them because they are not exactly what you expected. There is no need to wait for others to change our day. That person you care about so much, the person you talk to about everything, the person who loves you, the one you love but who doesn't reciprocate, your mother, your father, your boss, they will never give you the answer you want. Because you don't have to ask them, you must ask you, who is a different you every day.

# DO YOU KNOW WHAT REALLY CHANGED? EVERYTHING. MAINLY YOU; YOU ARE ANOTHER PERSON.

Contrary to what it might look like: I know that to this day you have not made jokes, that you fought, you fell down and you got up.

I know you tried to let slip what you couldn't change, that you experimented with and invented new ways of thinking.

You tried to help, you tried to give up, but you never made it anyway. You put on the armour, you wielded a weapon, then you said stop. You regained courage, you cried, you let yourself be overwhelmed by anger the moment before you stopped.

**Change is not easy, but you tried.**

You did it in solitude, hiding and healing your defeats like that soldier in the trenches we mentioned, who sews the shreds of his wounds alone, with a needle disinfected with Whisky.

Other times you asked for help, you received it, or you didn't. You tried to change clothes, u or haircut. You tried to show yourself as a new, different person, you tried to revolutionize and change the way others would see you. You tried to change things by changing yourself. You got married, you became a mother, now the kids are grown up or they are still small and sleeping in the other room. You have failed, you have succeeded, and you think you have never changed: you are not enough, you haven't made it. You felt such a pain you thought you would die. You stopped eating, you started drinking, then you stopped drinking and you started eating again. Too much. You followed manuals, bought books (*like this* one), saw tutorials, you tried to understand. You studied because you wanted to learn how to draw, to cook, to swim. You wanted to do many things and you still can't: that recipe is a mystery, the drawings are bad, you almost drowned in the water. You cannot, but your children do, your sisters do, your brothers do. You talked to your mother, you asked questions, and you got answers, but you didn't quite understand. Your father misses you every day and you miss not being able to ask him for help. Only he could help, but now it is too late. Now that you have made your bed, you have done the shopping and checked the bill, you have seen the money run out, one cent at a time. You were afraid, you were terrified, you cried surrounded by a darkness that seemed to never end. A darkness that ate everything, even the strength to go on again. You raised a white flag, you surrendered. No one answered and you thought the end had come. Someone came. Someone who looks like you, but who you don't recognize, who didn't think could be so similar to you and at the same time is not you.

*It is you and it is not you.*

The person waving the white flag and the hand that helps you get up, the battered soldier, the wrong drawing, the one word too many, the bewildered face:

**It is you, always** you.

And now you are here: time has passed, and you are here, still, despite everything. Look back and tell yourself one and only one thing: "thank you for accompanying me here."

*Because it is time you said hello, you are saying goodbye to it forever.*

"Even in the darkest moments, when everything seemed to be over, I was able to light a candle and one more candle, a candle every time, and I found the strength to stay one more day in this life."

*That is what you have to say to yourself, looking behind you, that is what I want you to say to the person you were.*

**Everything changed because I changed, I changed.**

"I, before anything else. First of all, first of everything, I'm still here, standing."

*And that is how you are going to say hello and thank that part of you that is gone, that you don't need anymore.*

Whenever you think you have failed, that you have done nothing, that you have not been anywhere, that you have not achieved any goals, you read these words, you close your eyes, you breathe and remember who you are.

*And let it go once and for all.*

Abandon this need to tell others what to do and what not to do, what is good and what is bad, what is right and what is wrong. Think of all the times someone has done it with you, when others judged you, told you what was right and what was not and how it made you feel: were you cornered, not understood. Can't you see how these are the two sides of the same coin? You cannot change others, just as others do not have the right to ask you to change. You do not have the right to ask others to do it either. You do not have to agree to change for others. You want change because in your mind you live in a fantasy world, you create it and then you overlap it with reality.

**Reality disappears and only the recurring, treacherous and deceptive fantasy remains that, eliminated a characteristic, curbed certain edge, changed a tiny aspect of the character, will change that person into a new person, perfect for you.**

Or you will be perfect for that person.

*Let go, say goodbye to the past.*

The fantasy that all misunderstandings, problems, pain between you and that person, father, mother, son, friend, companion, will end in the exact moment when that small, negligible, minimum, almost invisible detail will change.

*Unfortunately, we are a long way from the truth.*

It is never a small detail, negligible, minimal and invisible. You do not realize that speaking is your only Fear, that unhealthy terror of having to accept reality for what it is, accepting failure, the loss of the notorious control over things.

*Control, always control, when you should let go.*

Change is a long and difficult path, yet you pretend - how many times in a single day? That it is simple to convince someone to do so. Then you lose patience if the miracle does not happen. You get angry, you feel bad, you are disappointed if the magic doesn't happen. You don't understand how the other person doesn't get the importance, the simplicity, for the need to change.

*Yet you told them, repeated it over and over.*

If you really believe there needs to be a change, if you really think that things need to change, if you want things to change, you are the person who has to change.

*Now that you have said goodbye.*

And sometimes it might not even be enough to make a relationship that does not work, work. And if that is the case, There is not much else to do, nothing other than to leave. Just leave. Because a relationship can't be a prison. Ever.

*Starting with yourself.*
"But I know how tiring it has been to get here and I love you for it."

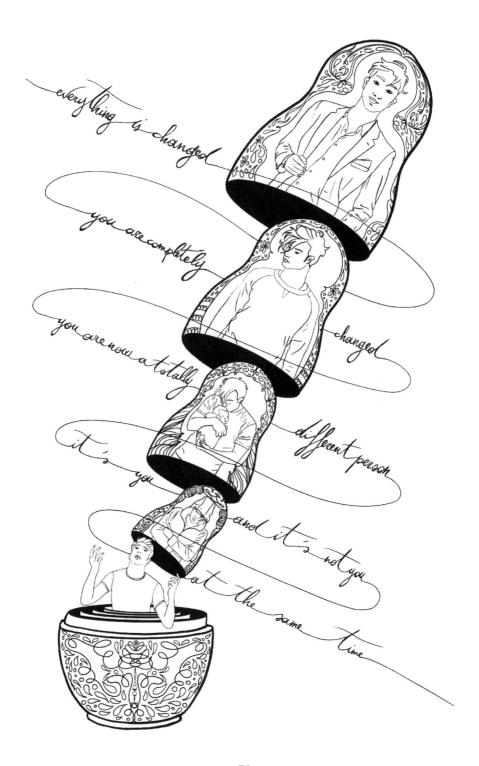

# ABOUT THE COUPLE

We just talked about relationships, about changing Others, we made a general speech about it, which can be applied to any area: from work, to family, to friendships. But one of the most difficult relationships to establish, maintain, build and maybe end is the one with the person you have chosen, the one next to you not because you have to and just happened to be there, but because you chose it, together *(hey, hello, if you are a kidnapper and you are reading, this chapter is not for you)*. Among relationships, this is one of the most difficult to manage for a number of reasons. First, we must remember every time those close to us are people who are completely alien to our family, who have not shared our journey, our education, our memories, which does not come from the same world. Almost like an alien who wasn't there the day before, and the next day we found ourselves in the kitchen, someone who didn't share their entire existence with us. This someone, this initial stranger, will become the person in whom we place our utmost and total trust. One of the few, if not the only person, we will allow to decide how we spend our time together, our money, our travels, our shopping, lunch and dinner, the daily routine. And it is a stranger. If you think about it, it comes like seasickness...

*What if things don't go the way I want to?*
*What if things go downhill at any moment?*

*What if he changes?*
*What if he doesn't love me?*
*What if he betrays me?*

The couple is the relationship that most exposes us to the risk of living completely open to a possible (and sometimes persecutory) future, without being more in the present: it puts our ability to be here and now, to a very hard test, dragging us into an unknown, murky and frightening future. For a long time, as you can see from the questions here above, which are likely to be yours, when you live in a couple relationship you risk not being here, in the present, now.

**You do not live the couple for what it is, but you swim in the anguish of the future.**

I must remind you that the future is a fantasy, it hasn't happened yet - otherwise what kind of future would it be – but one that comes at you with incredible force, like it is something real, that you can almost touch and for which you can certainly feel bad for. And if you are sick, what do you do? You defend yourself. Defending means acting, making decisions, moving on the board...in the wrong way. But why wrong?

*Because on the defensive, you can build an army, not a couple.*

Ask yourself, "Why is this person next to me?"

It could be because you need to remember to be better. Better than him, her, the whole world and every other living thing on planet earth, not just between men and women. So you can ask for help and get it without ever really asking for it.

*Getting help, may I remind you, is essential for you, but it should never be asked for, right?*

Asking for help would expose you, and therefore, you are better to avoid it: better to create this diabolical mechanism thanks to which without asking, you get.

We have already said this mechanism makes you indispensable, it ensures that you will never be injured, or abandoned

Does it work?
Small spoiler: No.

And to understand it is simple: think back to when you were a child. The Guilt, the control mechanisms your parents used with you, did they ever work? No, they never held anyone back.

*In fact, you are gone.*

Full of Guilt but far away. Or you remained, full of Guilt but unhappy. So, no: it doesn't work. People, in general, can't really hold you back. It may work for a while, but it can't hold up.
People at some point choose, freely. And even if they don't, if they were to be influenced by your words, your strategies, they wouldn't faithfully follow the path you printed in your mind. We are not robots, we do not carry out pre-arranged commands, we do not have predictable and controllable reactions.
Prompted by the same impulses, we react in a totally different, unpredictable way.

**To demand reactions is to feel wrong and Guilty whenever some-one does not meet our expectations.**

If this is your modus operandi, you do not want love, you do not seek love, you are not willing to work as a couple to get it, you just want confirmation of who you are, what you are, that you exist. You don't want someone to love: **you are just looking for someone who doesn't abandon you.** Look inside you again, look for your wounds. You have to look at your behavior, those of your mother and father, the origins that have forged you, the constant comparison with your brothers, sisters, friends. To them that they were always better than you. To you, you were never enough. How important it has become for you to seek perfection: so important that it becomes an engine generating failed events all the same to themselves.

**Not a stimulus, but a chain.**

Why?

Because maybe one day you opened your heart and it didn't go as you expected. Because maybe you waited days for them to write to you, to call you, to come back to love you, to come back and want you. But he or she does not come back, they do not call, they have not changed, and they are not looking for you. They do not care about the efforts you have made, the ones you are going to make, they are not interested in getting *better.* they do not care you have become better.

**Better for whom, then?**

I must be tough here: **stop waiting for someone to love you in your stead.** May someone one day decide to give you all the love you cannot give yourself. Someone who, you do not even know how, can make you feel like the right person in the right place.

*A kind of magician, an illusionist who can love you, bring out the best in you and make you understand once and for all that you are in the right place.*

Do not wait for someone to come back just because you have reacted, because you have changed because you are not the same person anymore. They will not start loving you like magic. Trying to fill a void that does not belong to them, which they will never even remotely fill.

**Your emptiness is not their place.**

You try to replace them with your parents, with those who may not have loved you as they should or do not love you at all, those who hurt you, and that you finally - unlike them - believe that you can change, in the right place, with the love you think you deserve, in the time, ways and quantities you think are right for you.

*You are getting revenge.*
*You are deluding yourself.*
*You are still hurting.*

Giving someone a role that does not belong to them, mortifying them in a battle that does not involve them, putting the same table tokens in for different games. You are not fair to yourself, regarding your past and the person you would like by your side. You are not the problem, believe me. The problem is not you who are not enough, trust me.

Do not think about it anymore, otherwise you will never see the real problem. The real problem lies in the fact that you can only identify love as something to be fixed. Outside of you, of course.

# EVEN SCREAMING AND BEGGING YOU WILL NEVER CHANGE THEM, NOR WILL YOU LET THEM LOVE YOU.

So, you spend your time desperately trying to change someone you have chosen for some purely random reason. And you find yourself in solitude and despondency, alone with the Fear of being wrong. You are surrounded by things that do not exist: moments of confusion, pauses of reflection, ultimatums.

*But you are not at war.*

You are not a hostage; it is not worth forcing yourself to live like this. **But there is a war,** it really exists, and it is inside you: in your head, you fight, every moment, every day and fall prisoner to your desires. They get stuck, paralyzed, like during a tennis match when left with the ball in your hands, unsure whether to serve or not. **You wait, but you do not even know what for.**

There is no point in waiting.

**You cannot think of giving others exactly what they need, you do not have to think about giving others what you need.**

Because there is a very powerful filter between reality and what you believe is reality: you.

**You are the filter with which you look at the real and confuse it.**

Your experiences, your feelings, your emotions, your training, your life. Every single aspect of your life, from when you were born to the moment you read these words.

*Your life up till here.*

You can take care of someone; you can look after someone, you can do it to the best of your ability, and I don't question it. I am sure you have already done it; you are doing it and it is an excellent job, but That is not going to turn you into a magician who can read thoughts and give someone what they need.

*Not even if you want it that much.* Because you think it would finally make you happy.

<u>**Taking care of others does not mean giving others everything you have, in a totalizing, exclusive action.**</u>

What I have described is not love. It is a request. A desperate request you make to the other person, hiding it under miles of expectations and pounds of homemade cakes. You ask to receive love, to finally be appreciated, to receive applause, compliments, gifts, recognition only because you have moved your border a little further every day. One centimeter at a time to satisfy the desires of the other, the needs of the other, the needs of the other. All things that exist only in your head. They never asked, and you chose them just because they needed you. And if you have someone next to you who asks you to advance, who demands it without even asking, if someone forces you to always step forward: that person is toxic. Messing with you and your life, your way of doing it, just because it is convenient for them. Because even your significant other believes that they are not enough and in your progression, they will find dissatisfaction, loss of self-esteem, lack of realization. And That is where they want you to be. On the fence. Where nothing has to change, everything is immutable, everything is wrong and in its perfect imperfection to complain.

## Being able to complain is essential for not changing.

So, you create a vicious circle in which you do everything, and you are thrilled to do it because it makes you feel like you are worth it. A vicious circle in which the other retreats, without a road to fall back on, where you do everything yourself, living a relationship where their viewpoint is not important enough and where they cannot look after themselves. Because you stop them. Because you do everything in their stead. But it doesn't make any sense, does it? It could be your desk mate you have always fancied, your wife, your children - now able to understand and want - your colleagues, your boss. You are convinced that you must decide and act for others too, when your duty is limited to yourself: to decide what is right and what is wrong for you. *Just for you.*

## In a relationship, borders are fundamental.

Just imagining that someone can finally love you because you have completely erased yourself in exchange for love is emotional suicide.

**Doing everything for everyone won't make you loved, it is not an equation.**

It is not enough to climb on the cross and ask to start with the nails, the crown of thorns and all the rest.

*If it was not enough for the son of God to be loved by the whole of humanity, it will certainly not be enough for you.*

But you don't want to be crucified anymore, right? Instead, you want to try to understand where the void lies within you and that you are trying to fill. And That is what we are doing, slowly, slowly. If you like the person you are dating, you think you love them, but you don't think they are behaving the way you want it to; If it hurts you, if it is not *exactly* how you imagined it, I'll tell you one thing: you are not ready for a relationship yet.

**Not with this person, nor with another.**

Not now, not now, not in these conditions, not like that. Because it won't work. That person is not what you want. Your mother doesn't like him. He doesn't convince your father. He is not there when you want to celebrate. He leaves you alone. He forced you to give up everything and everyone just to have time him.

*Excuses, all excuses.*

That is not why it didn't work, it can't work, it won't work. You don't want that relationship, and not even another one. Let's see: let's say that I'm right, and that you don't want a relationship, just to be loved.

*If that were the case, what would you do?*

You'd think that by talking, screaming, writing, explaining, you'd be able to get people to change their minds. To convince even those who don't love you to take that one place next to you. A random person, chosen because maybe that afternoon you felt lucky, a person who still does not know that has been chosen with a single purpose: to give you all the love you want. You think you just need to explain who you are and what you want, and people will magically begin to love you. That is why you don't spare yourself, you stick to long explanations, endless messages, you keep insisting because you believe that if that person finally understood who you really are, they could do nothing but love you. You are ready to convince them that you will give up everything, that you will never need anything, that you will settle. To have them by your side. You keep forgetting that you are not the other person. That you can do nothing to make them love you, that you don't have to.

**You can't convince anyone to love you.**

*Not the ones who left you or who you haven't met yet.*

That is not how love works. That is why you are not ready for a relationship, *because you still don't know what love* is. You are looking for something That is not there, you are looking for it in the wrong place, you'll never find the keys in that drawer that weren't there a minute ago, imagine what you need.

**Love means acceptance, surrender and passion.**

*The acceptance of oneself and others, surrendering to the feeling and passion in building day after day what until the day before was only our own: life.*

Where to start? With you. You are the first person you must love in your life. Look inside yourself with a feeling of acceptance, surrendering to who you are and to your feelings and with passion let yourself go every day to reach it: look inside you and protect yourself, caress your heart and say one thing only: *I love you. You are the most important person in my life.*

# ABOUT UPS AND DOWNS

I have not yet scratched the surface of your judgmental part, here it is: you believe that you no longer have time, that now what is done is done, that if you could be reborn you would listen to me, that you would suggest this book to your youngest friend, to your children, to your colleague, because it will work for anyone but you. It is too late for you and you would rather stay and suffer. You think that by now, that is your character, you are in a couple and you don't want to throw it all away. Your friends are happier because they were luckier, your kids are grown up now, your parents are old. There is nothing more you can do, you can't leave, you can't change them, and you can't change. I even said that. You Repeat to yourself that if you left for somewhere else, you would not be able to find anyone who wants you, no one with whom to spend time. You tell yourself that all in all the situation has only *ups and downs*, which is normal. How often have I heard this sentence and how often have I repeated it to myself, I understand you, but it is not so.

**A relationship has no ups and downs.**
**A family has no ups and downs.**

With this, I am not telling you that life does not have surprises, even so difficult to deal with. I would live on another planet if I thought so, on the contrary, I just want to invite you to think of the couple, the family, relationships - in general - as something you have chosen. And if you chose to be with someone, to share the way, to go somewhere, to chase a job, to design a dream, the difficulties must also be part of the *ups*. In our hearts, in our thoughts, even when we encounter a problem, we should see it as an opportunity to be who we are, to pursue what we have chosen, to live like the couple we have created.

Every opportunity is an opportunity to remember who we are, to see realized our true essence, to play with our being and shape it as best we can. Adapting to reality, to its needs, to the other and to their desires, to our brothers, sisters, parents. Keeping the idea of ourselves firmly in place.

I know what you are thinking: that all this is a utopia, that you just have to settle because a family has so many pluses, so *what is the problem with those two, three flaws? Are you sure?*

# BE WHOEVER YOU WANT TO BE.

That doesn't mean being settled. When I was talking about adapting, I meant compromise. Because *in life you have to compromise, not settle,* you are not alone in a castle in the middle of nowhere. There are our needs and those of Others, our desires and those of our companion in adventures. In life, we always decide who will take the garbage out, who will take the dog for a walk, who will look after the children, who will take care of those who are sick. In joy and struggle, in all situations. In those famous ups *and downs,* that actually are not as such.

**You always meet in the middle.**

But no, *you do not settle for* it. It is not necessary.

Once again, you have to replace a few words, tear down the veil that does not let you observe things for what they are. Because if you are content, if yours aren't compromises but sacrifices, if you are putting yourself aside for each other, if you are stepping back too much, if you are moving too far, we've already talked about it: you are in a situation that has only one name, a toxic relationship. And you could get into such a relationship even with yourself, not respecting yourself, not leaving yourself the possibility to take the form you prefer but limiting yourself to a faded design that no longer belongs to you. Do not do that. You are wasting your only one life, and you have to take that into account. When something is *difficult* and the *difficulty* is your ability to make sensible decisions, then this is not difficult: it is just **challenging.** See the words and how perceptions change? A challenging thing is not an impossible thing, unfeasible, unattainable, no. A challenging thing is just one thing that requires commitment, that is all. Commitment for you, for the people you love, for your desires, dreams and goals.

**I never said it would be easy but it is great to be free.**

You can't and don't even have to imagine spending even just one day of your life, so precious and unique, with someone you don't want, who doesn't love you, who doesn't want you. You can't and shouldn't even imagine spending another day in that office you don't like, doing a job that doesn't make you happy, accepting sacrifices that betray yourself and who you are.

Imagine having a sheet of paper and some scissors and cutting out a square. Imagine looking at it. What is it? A simple square if left on the table. That is its nature, and it seems impossible to make it change its face. But if you decide to make it into origami, you will see its forms multiply indefinitely. As you can give that sheet of paper endless possibilities to be, imagine how many things you can do with yourself.

**But you are not a sheet of paper but a human being.**

You are not flat and thin, you have a thousand nuances, emotions and desires within you. See? There are endless possibilities to be happy and they are waiting for you **beyond your Fear.**

# ABOUT LEAVING

If it is difficult to accept that we have to leave, to get out of a wrong, and toxic relationship where we do not belong, it will be even more difficult to accept that someone has decided to leave before us. Maybe without explanation, without saying a word. Or they explained it to us, but we pretended not to understand, not to see, not to hear. We have persisted in chasing something that was no longer there and even now that it is over, we read the messages, we think about the things that were said and not said, the things we did and the things we would have liked to do. We continue to live by imagining that we have a person who is actually not there, pretending and tricking us into being part of a life that not only does not belong to us, but that does not even touch us.

*We have to start with ourselves if we want things to really change and stop hurting us.*

Ask yourself, "Am I still able to forgive?"

Looking in the mirror, can you put aside your disappointment, anger, despondency and forgive yourself?

**Because to forgive any other person, you must first be able to forgive yourself.**

How do you forgive? How can you forgive? Going beyond failure, one's first: that of others comes later. And That is why when I tell you to forgive, I invite you to forgive yourself first. To face yourself first, you have to start from there. **From your own failures.** Because you think you failed, don't you? You can't accept that what you did, chosen, that what happened at a certain moment, something that might even be happening right now, in this very moment, is the only chance you could have chosen from the thousand infinite possibilities, right? But now you know, time does not exist: there is no other time than this moment, your decision-making skills are (and always have been) at the maximum of their potential, you have always chosen as best you could, you have always done your best. Now you know. Do not let Fear overwhelm you, it is the Fear of change that tells you this isn't true. And you do not like being subjected to Fear anymore, I know. The role you have played so far is only one: *the* victim. The victim is the only character you have allowed yourself to act to the fullest.

*What role is more stable, predictable, repetitive than that of the victim?*

It is not scary, is it?

And then every victim has their own executioner: there is always the villain on duty, the monster, the enemy, the one who does not allow you to be free, who does not let you live, that prevents you from being happy.

**The executioner is always to blame.**

That Guilt you do not have. Ever.

92

*We live in a society that helps us become victims.*

The victims remain silent, does not rebel, at most they cry and complain. Victims do not change, they don't innovate, they don't ask for anything. Only to be understood and pitied:
Like you.
It is easy to govern the victims.

*Do you want to be a victim now?* **Or take your responsibility.**

The fault is all in your head and helps you create worlds that does not exist. *Just like when you cannot accept that things are over between you, that it went as it was supposed to.* It did not work, you say. Repeat you broke up and people will ask you sooner or later "who is to blame?" You will answer they are to blame, if you want to play the role of the victim. *Mine,* if you want to bask in Guilt. But what if you did not break *up?* If, like all human beings, do sooner or later: *did you just change your mind? Because* things do not always go as we imagined.

# IF I JUST START SAYING "WE CHANGED OUR MINDS" INSTEAD OF "WE BROKE UP."

Think about it every time you say *we broke up and left each other.* But go where, exactly? Where are you now? Where you were left.

If you tell me, I swear I'm coming to get you. Give me an address, send me the location, let me know where you are.

*You don't tell me because you can't.*

You can't because the place where you *broke up* doesn't exist in space, but only in time.

**You have broken up at a point of time, not space.**

And that is why it hurts so much. Because you have stayed there, in a place that can no longer exist because it belongs in the past.

*You are with the apple now.*

But you do not have to be, because unlike the apple, which is just a memory, you belong to today and you must stop wondering what you could have done or said differently. You must stop imagining *how things would turn out if...*

**Things could go no other way.**

We repeat it again:

**things went the only way they could.**

What you have already experienced, that is in the past and that no longer exists. Give a rest to your mind, honor your choices: they were the only things you could have done at that moment. Not now, not with the awareness of the future, not in another way, in another time, as if you were a different person. At that moment, with those experiences, it was all you could do. You must make peace with this concept. It is your job. Now that you are not together anymore, you are not frozen and you are still alive.

## Because no one is unreplaceable

The only unreplaceable person is you, the only person you couldn't live without is you, you and no one else. So, if by any chance you are still thinking about it, if There is actually someone next to you right now and you look at them and you think There is nothing left to say or do, listen. Do not even think for a moment *you are* breaking up.

## Because people do not just leave, just as people do not belong to each other.

*At most people choose each other.*

And it is a choice that must be made every day, every morning, every night, for good and evil, with money or without, with hope or without but you choose. With children, without children, with lovers, without lovers, with friends, without friends, with family, without family. *Choosing, nothing else.*

Because two people who are together and share their way have chosen to stay together, they have chosen to be together, they have chosen to help each other, they have chosen to make themselves happy, they have chosen to love each other.

Everything else does not exist, it doesn't matter. And if you were still wondering:

*what happens when you do not choose anymore?*
Well, **you do not break up, you just change your way.**

And you do not need any closure, just to change your ways. To leave. You need to end something, but inside you and not outside of you. To end it for real, to accept that that time is over, that that person will no longer be there. You do not need to *break up permanently* with anyone. If a story is over, if a friend is gone, if the most important person in your life has walked away, if someone has *changed their mind*, you don't need to chase after them to tell them - and tell you - that you have to end it together. It is not what you are looking for, it is not a definitive end.

**When you tell yourself that you need a story to end, you really just want answers.**

Why did you leave me? Why wasn't I enough? Why wasn't I good enough for this job? Why don't you want to talk to me anymore? Why don't you want to be my friend anymore? Why did you disappear? Why don't you call me? Why didn't you look for me anymore? Why didn't you show up again? Why don't you give me another chance? An endless, unanswered collection. You just want to know why. You are convinced that if I could talk to them, they would still understand. you even hope that perhaps looking at you might change your mind, realize that you have made a mistake. May the mere fact of seeing on one another help to remember, to rebuild your relationship remember how magnificent you were. That you will return to each other's life. And why do you think that? Because your biggest Fear is not hanging out with that person anymore, working in that office, having a beer with that friend of yours, confiding in you, listening, talking, laughing. No, your greatest Fear belongs to the memory.

*You tremble at the idea that walking away means forgetting.*

You have a tremendous Fear of being or just becoming a shadow.

# THERE IS NO DEFINITIVE END THAT YOU NEED.

Your most painful thought is that he/she has already forgotten how capable you were, how good it was to laugh with you, to be with you, to talk to you. You are afraid that your boss has already forgotten how good your work was, indispensable, fundamental, how prepared you were in the industry, how fast you were at solving problems, how useful, attentive, the importance of your judgments, advice, thoughts. You are afraid that all this will disappear, that your merits will be forgotten, that what is good has vanished.

*Because you would disappear, too.*

And you are sure that by reviewing, talking about it, all this would come back to light, clear and obvious, the other would admit and instantly recognize their error.

*Your place would be safe.*
*Your memory also.*

But it is not reality. And the reason is not what you believe: not because you are not worth enough. It is not your fault those people have not stayed in your life, it is not your fault for changing jobs.

97

**You are perfect and deserving of all the love you can get.**

And That is the only thing you need to think about. Every morning. Every night. Breathe and remember that you are deserving of every drop of love in the world.

The day you were given life, you already had within you every possible happiness, every ability, every characteristic, every merit, every kindness, genius, courage, piece to achieve and be all you desire. If it is not your fault, whose is it, then? Theirs? No, not even theirs.

*There is no fault.*

And the reason those people are no longer part of your life is that they *were not your people.*

**They were not your people.**

Repeat it again.

*They were not my people.*

You do not need to hear anything from them because it is not closure you seek but unconditional love, acceptance above all else, and a gratification for every effort you have made. And for all these things there is only one person in the world who can give them to you: yourself. And we have already begun to figure out how, right? Listening to yourself, reading yourself, knowing where the emotions start, forgiving yourself, slowly discovering who you are and how you are and, now lowering, the Guilt. Stop suffering again and again, every day, if that person is gone, if they chose to be without you. They do not love you, it is a certainty, a reality. You know it, your friends know it, even your mother told you. Everybody knows it, and you know it too. They do not love you; they do not want you and they do not want to be with you.

*Then why are you still suffering?*

Because you think it is your fault, that you could have done something different, but it is not true. You cannot change what is inside someone else's head. Even if sometimes it seems possible, it is not.

*Even if you are sometimes convinced you did or felt like you did, you know it is not true.*

People do not convince themselves, even by taking responsibility that does not exist. Repeat with me: *it is not my* fault. **It is not my fault.**

# IT IS NOT YOUR FAULT FOR ANYONE WHO DOESN'T LOVE YOU OR DIDN'T LOVE YOU

It is not and never will be. It is not your fault and you can do nothing about it even if you wanted to. Even if you chose that person and now you do not want to start over. Even if you think you love them. True, it can be frustrating, and the mere thought of starting over gives you chills.

A movie comes up to my mind, "Sorry for *the delay*" (a film by and with Massimo Troisi, rest his soul), the scene in which Tonino ima- gines a new beginning: after days of crying, moaning, despair, after wondering where he had gone wrong and what he had done wrong, convinced by friends, he tries to move on. And where does it stop? He thinks about the sauce with "pellecchie" (which would be the skins of tomatoes). He does not like it; he never liked the sauce done that way and before he convinced his ex-girlfriend to prepare it dif- ferently, it took months. Now, the idea of starting over with another, eating for months and months the *skins*, before she learns, makes him change his mind about it.

*The mere idea of starting over, of explaining, of understanding another person is scary.*

And that is right, each of us has our own *tomato skins*, and being with someone means understanding each other a little bit at a time. Be- cause we are strangers, remember? But this is also the beauty of it, experimenting, learning, building. So, stop complaining, stop hiding behind a love that no longer exists (did it ever really exist?). They are screens, defenses.

*Never say you cannot love anyone like you have already loved.*

That is the unconscious. And what do we tell them unconscious? *Not today*. Love is light, mild and kind. Love should have to make you feel full and not empty, and I, who found love after I hurt myself in every way possible, I can swear to you. I was betrayed, I was aban- doned, I was hurt before I gave up, but I gave up. I let it go and let the ship sail freely and I did not try to keep the pieces of a bad story together. I only kept the shards (because those shards were *me*).

**And unexpectedly someone fell in love with it.**

Someone who has not let me go for a second since that day. Not one. Someone who took my flaws and made them jewelry. Someone who has seen the beautiful things in me and considered them excellent. Someone who looks at everything I do, I say and think with tenderness, understanding and respect. This is love. And you know it. You just do not want it yet. Why? Because you are still like Tonino. You are still here wondering why she left you, the one who made the wrong sauce. Then maybe it is better to take a few more steps in solitude and understand together there is nothing to know, nothing to understand, nothing to discover. No truth that will change your day, no incredible discovery that will finally make it all clear.

I started by saying this is not a book of magic.

But you are already making a plan, slowly.
And now let us see how.

# KNOWING SOMEONE'S MOTIVES WILL NOT MAKE THEIR ACTIONS MORE ACCEPTABLE.

Knowing will not solve your Fears, then do yourself a favor: stop asking. Stop repeating to you and those around you that "you just need to know why." You do not need to know why, that is not what you are really asking. You are once again hiding your Fear of not being worthy enough and confronting those who hurt you, asking them why they did it, you need to pander to it. Embrace the Fear of not being and hope that comparison will disprove it. You expect that person - who has already said that they do not love you, who has already shown that they do not want to be with you - will tell you that love is possible, it is easy, it is beautiful. But you do not realize that they are the least fit person. If it were right to ask someone, you or them, they would be the last people to question.

There is no *closure*, no. *Final speech* because we are not in a movie, there is no need for a plot twist, there is no need for an author's dialogue that causes you to tear up with an applause.

## There is no comparison that can cure your wounds.

The most the other person could do is to tell you *I know it is my fault* and then add phrases like, but *I can't help it.* It happens to everyone and it hurts. Your life is your responsibility and to heal, you must decide that you want to heal. Stop watching things happen and ask yourself, *"Why do I feel that way? Why does this scare me so much? Who do I have to prove this to?"* The right answer is: to no one, I tell you. But before you get to that answer to understand why you are doing it, and I know you have every way to do it. This is your little miracle, your magic today.

*And* the *other?*

Their path and their battle have nothing to do with yours anymore. No more.

**And by your choice, not theirs.**

# ABOUT THE DESIRE FOR BEING LIKED

There is something that unites the pages we've gone through, a general sense that binds me, you and everyone who's going to read this book. A phrase that has accompanied us, a conviction that I hope you will abandon very soon (if you have not already done so, and in that case, I am proud of you)

The catchphrase that runs through the centuries:
*"If the others like me, then I'm fine."*.

But is there really anyone or something that everyone might like? No. There is definitely something you like more than any other, something that you consider absolutely the best, the most beautiful.

Something that you think should be appreciated by everyone.

But I bet you have already met at least one person who said, "I don't like it."

"How is that possible?" you will have found yourself thinking.

"That is the absolute best thing in the world and you don't like it, what is on your mind?"

Same as I think when someone tells me they don't like ice cream. *Let's face it*, there are people who don't like ice cream.

**To please everyone not even being born an ice cream would have been enough**.

Because there are a thousand tastes, there are those who prefer those fruit flavoured (*crazy*), others the variations of chocolate, some cream with inside the pieces of something special (like me) and there are those who loathe it in any form, taste and colour. Because what you like doesn't necessarily appeal to Others. Because that is your truth, not Others 'truth.

*Nothing is absolute, not even ice cream!*

You know that, rationally, but you keep thinking that if you don't like you all, then there should be something wrong with you.

"*Is it possible that no one finds anything interesting in me?* " is the question you ask yourself and every time you find a different answer. First, it is the nose fault: maybe it is too big. Then it is the money: not enough. Maybe you are not that smart. Or in relationships, you demand too much (or too little, you underestimate yourself) and others run away. Even your friends have stopped calling you, they don't go out with you anymore because they are so much prettier.

*They go to the gym, you don't go.*
*They are single, you haven't been that for a while.*
*They don't have children, you do.*
*Your friends play football but you don't because you can't.*
*They go to the disco, but you can't dance.*

*They are having fun, and you are not.*
*Others do everything, they work, they study, they do everything better than you.*
*Others are liked by everyone, and they are happy.*

Are there any other false visions of life you want to invent to convince yourself that you are right not to get out of your little walnut shell? You tell a truth every day, you find something you don't do and should do, something you don't have and that you should have, something you are not and should be. You repeat yourself that you lost at the start, that you will never reach them: because until you get your nose fixed or you will earn more or you will take that specialization course or you will change your wardrobe or your children will be grown or will meet someone who is worth it, until then there will be nothing you can do but stay where you are, in front of a white wall, complaining.

*Terrible.*

Nothing of the last lines is true, nothing you repeat until nausea exists and do not even begin with the usual "but me, but him, but them, but her..." because if you have come or gone here it is because what you read is *awakening* you. Nothing you think about yourself is true, nothing you imagine about others is true.

**You are not that *bad*; they are not so *good*.**

The reality you have painted is unfair to you and excessively lenient in theirs. But Others, believe me, don't care. When you repeat that you have to please everyone, when you worry about anyone's opinion, when you compare yourself to this and that, you actually have a specific person in mind.

**You don't want to please everyone.**

*You want to please your mom or dad who never made you feel enough and never gave you a place to lean on.*

So, you never got to understand how much you were worth, except in your reflection in Others 'eyes. And you know what? You will live a lot longer than them, and you can't change their minds. And do you want to know something else?

## <u>You don't need their approval; you just need yours.</u>

We have seen this in previous chapters: learning not to control Others, to listen to oneself, to know how to let go. Your others are not just any other people, but you will have to learn to react the same way.

*Defuse expectations. Stop acting to make them happy.*

Teach your Unconscious to take another path. In life, there are, and always will be (everyday), people with whom we will share time and space but not by choice. Maybe people who will have to be part of our lives but who we would have loved never to meet. You have prepared clear and defined images of how these people are made, how they reason, how they choose and why they choose A instead of B. Those people become bits of you, of your ideas and you think you *understand* them. You demand, with your reasoning, with your own struggle, with that immense effort you do every time, to understand others through your experience and your knowledge. As if others were made of your own *experience*. You actually do this with anyone, not just those who make you feel uncomfortable, but there is a special reason I talked about them. I did it to make it clearer that you don't really question Others, you don't care about other people's opinions, otherwise, you should be able to balance both those who think well of you and those who think badly of you, almost undoing the account. You reason, you investigate, you are surprised that you are looking for another truth.

*Where did I go wrong? Why am I wrong? Why doesn't that person love me? Why doesn't that person talk to me? What can I do to keep me from hating myself? How can I be appreciated by those who speak ill of me?*

These are questions that remind you of something, right? This is why I talked about people you don't get along with. But it is a reasoning you can apply to anyone. You always try to please others and when you can't ask these questions, these doubts, which are born and live mostly independently, become balls of fire and go up at the throat. The questions you ask are always the same. You are not looking for the truth, you are not investigating plausible reasons for misunderstanding:

*you have already assumed that the mistake is theirs, but the fault is yours.*

The questions you ask are always the same since when you were at school and you asked yourself, "Why don't they want me? Why don't you want to be my friend? Why doesn't he/she talk to me? Why they don't like me"

And the answer is one: **because you don't like yourself.**

But that is not the answer to any of your questions. That is the answer to the one question you should ask and actually never ask yourself. Throw in the litter bin all the questions you have read so far and you usually ask, erase them from this book with a pen, delete them from your mind and just ask yourself.

*"Why does this make me suffer?"*

It doesn't matter who is on the other side, which the nature of who *hates* you, the haters you have collected, how many they are and where they come from, their reputation or how reason. Whoever they are, whatever their number, whatever their face, the question to be asked is always the same, same as the answer. What matters is knowing which stand you are coping with yourself, not what other people are thinking. What matters is why you are still suffering and what you are doing with your day right now, in this very moment. What matters is to be aware of yourself while you breathe. Because *you are breathing, right?* I know you never notice. You have to be clear at what point you are in considering yourself *unique* and *perfect, without exceptions.*

**Unique and perfect, without exceptions.**

Otherwise, you will always remain to reason about someone, to give time and energy to those who exist only in your head, taking them away from the most important person of all: you.

# ARE NOT YOURS THEIR AUBERGINES

The heart of the question is always the same: someone makes you angry, either it makes you sad or humiliates you or makes you ashamed. And you can't stand it. Try to imagine life as a big supermarket in which you are the last customer who has just crossed the automatic door. In front of you, there are endless possibilities, shops of all kinds, goods of all kinds, there are opportunities for all tastes and for all wallets. But you don't know what you want yet, you don't know what you are looking for, you have just entered and it is only right that you should be given time to understand, to evaluate, to choose. Others, the ones that interact in your life, are a bit like the salesmen, the managers, the salespeople of all those stores in front of you. You can't buy from each one, you can't buy everything. You would spend more than you have, you would consume all your energy because the exchange currency is made of love, emotions, time. You can't even think of going into a store and just because you came in to look around, you feel obliged to buy something just because you disturbed the saleswoman or the salesman. You should end up with an endless series of junk, little things, you buy just so you don't displease Others, but you don't really need them. You did it because you wanted to please all the clerks who greeted you kindly. You are convinced that if you didn't do it, they would treat you superciliously. Let's pretend, then, that they do. What is going on with you? You feel bad about it. Even just for a moment. Just because you are telling yourself, "It is not fair." You cannot think that it was the sales assistant, the same guy who tried to sell you anything until a moment ago, to fail. He couldn't make you appreciate what was in his store. Why? Because you are in complete control of what you like and what you don't.

*But it is not enough for you.*

111

When you realize that they look at you badly, that they respond to you coldly, when you sense they may have changed their mind about you, then you feel the despondency or anger grow, the sadness invaded you, the frustration burning. Do you lose control? Maybe. And instead of walking out of the store, you blame the people in front: they hurt you, they hit you. And repeat phrases like "They should tell me what they think of me, why didn't anyone come to tell me?" or "They say this and that, but nothing is true," and "if he (or she) behaves like this, it is normal for me to react like that" or "I only do it for the kids." But there is only one child you are trying to protect and justify: you.

## What others say about you doesn't have to make you suffer

You don't have to look at them to figure out how to put them back in their place. You don't have to prepare for any challenges and no fight. You have to look in the mirror and see if you are in the right place, with the right people and in the right store. No one ever forced you to buy that dress, those shoes or those aubergines. You may not want aubergine. And if you don't have *it*, *very well*, go away! Do not let yourself be conditioned by those who do not know you, who do not even know the context, everything that is around you and inside your head. From the saleswoman to the store manager, from your mother to the fourth-grade aunt, someone will always be convinced that they know what is right or better for you, there will always be someone with an indispensable opinion. About you, what you do, who you are. Why? Because it is easy, isn't it?

*It costs no effort.*

Judging other people is so simple and costs nothing. And what costs nothing, neither effort nor money, is within anyone reach. Of anyone, and you forget this.

**Everyone can judge you.**
And you don't distinguish amongst the people are speaking, you don't think "that person knows me, he is trustworthy" or "that person doesn't know anything about me," you just see a hint of your fault to give up and say, "That person is right." You only have to see them come from afar to capitulate because they have triggered your Fears, your Fears are true and if someone else says them out loud then it is a confirmation.

**You have your Fears confirmed from the outside and you take them back into reality.**

You forget that all this doesn't matter; what does matter is just how you handle your reaction to their words.

**To their opinions.**

You don't give any weight to the work you do every day to stay afloat, to grow up, to be happy. You allow others to sabotage you, you surrender to anyone's words. Just a look of *this* or a half-sentence of *that* and everything collapses. Why is that?

*Because even this is easy, of course.*

It takes courage and effort to achieve goals, even if they are now before your eyes and it would be enough to extend your hand to grasp them. It takes energy not to listen to the Fear inside you that repeats,

"You will not make it" even when you have already made it. It would be enough to continue for a while and instead, the tiniest gust of wind is enough to wipe you out rolling backwards at the beginning of the journey. Just enough to find an excuse and never continue. Surrender and blame bad luck and Others, repeating "I'm not enough, anyway" and give everything up.

**But you have all the cards to get where you want, all of them. You were born that way.**

You can believe the lies of people do not know you, you can let yourself be moved from the headwind, or you can trust yourself and repeat to yourself:

*I have everything I need to be loved, to have everything beautiful in this life and I will allow no one to question it today.*

And today **is every day.**

# ABOUT MAKING THE IMPOSSIBLE REAL

We are halfway through our journey and I'm sure getting here wasn't easy: you have experienced confusion, enthusiasm, Fear and the desire to move on. All at the same time. You have probably thought about sending some of these phrases to a person. It doesn't matter who, it doesn't matter when and it doesn't even matter how close you are to this someone and we don't even know where he is and what he is doing but he is out there. You do it because you know these words tell the truth, that they can help you, but you prefer them to be comforting someone else first. That they are the key to change that person, but not yourself. Not yet. To avoid change in any way, the Unconscious defends its own system (i.e., the today you) by holding your hands and feet tied up to your mind and the things you believe you want.

*If they were really the things you want, you should be free.*

Instead, you are trapped in. Why? Because the distance between your true desires (happiness, freedom, courage, absence of Fear, anxiety, anguish) and the desires of your survival (recognition and constant certification of the self, desire to be recognized, cared for, appreciated) are the miles you have to walk from here to the day when you will be free. For real. Don't be unfair, don't blame yourself too much: this sense of oppression that crushes you, that follows you with every step and every breath, belongs to you and thousands of other people who also (from the outside) seem perfect, complete, accomplished and smiling. Change is for everyone the most difficult thing that exists, yet the most natural to adapt to life. You are working on it, and I couldn't be prouder.

# LOVE ME, PLEASE.

This is the phrase you want or do not want, consciously or unconsciously, screaming it or in a low voice, saying it or hiding it, you have repeated more than any other phrase throughout your life. And, as you have seen, it is a concept. As you could see, I have discussed this several times already: your desire to be loved This is the most difficult of the phrases you will encounter in this book, it is the phrase that must no longer be born spontaneously under your skin. The brand you have and needs to fade, the lyricist who has to change job. This sentence, if all goes well, we will never say it again. You will hear it only from one heart: yours. That he is looking at you, like Julia Roberts did with Hugh Grant in *Notting Hill*, and he is asking you to love him. You are wasting your time talking to someone else. Your dream, your desire, your need, your will and your project. The house you want, the job you are chasing, the degree, the exam, the perfect relationship. Instead of focusing on what you want and making it clear in front of you, perfectly polished, every day, you have been complaining about it and talking about it left and right because the approval of others to you has been more important than the thing itself. You talked about it, but you didn't focus on making it happen.

Yours was a mechanism that kept you safe, doing nothing, without having to do anything.

*You may have noticed that I am talking about the past.*

You have exposed yourself to the judgment of those who cannot or do not want to help you, you have also spoken to those who had no interest in seeing you reach your goals: you have forced yourself to suffer in the lack of what you wanted, hiding behind the criticisms of people judging you or the silence of those ignoring you. To the lack of support from people not believing in you. Who didn't give you trust.

I have been often listening, I do not know how many times, friends, speaking badly of their boss, to say the worst things and to add, candidly, as if it were the most normal thing in the world, "But is it not absurd that he entrusts some tasks to others and not to me? Isn't it absurd that he prefers those toadies to me?" No, it is not at all absurd that a person who doesn't have your esteem - and doesn't have it because you envy their position - prefers the company of others to yours. And no, not necessarily others are toadies if they can make that other person feel better than you do, than how you feel.

*I know, it is a scold.*

But there are things you can change: your attitude towards goals, just to begin with. Thence I spoke in past tense because I know that we are already a step ahead with the awareness of your love for yourself and now we can act. **Stop complaining,** stop saying you don't do what you should do just because you don't have what you need. To surround yourself with people you don't value, who you don't appreciate, for whom every gesture is an incredible effort.

**You are all you need to get wherever you want.**

Go get that relationship, that damn degree, the master, the job, buy the house, earn more, seize your life. Do it on your own and focusing only on you. Yes.

*Never forget that you are someone else opportunity too.*

Not of all, of course, but of those who can and wants the impossible, just like you. And you will be a bright beacon for them all, once you have taken your time and your energies to get where you want. And don't think relying on someone is wrong or embarrassing. Think about when you were the one who was supportive, when a smile depended on your gesture or you wiped away a tear, you hugged someone. The most beautiful feeling in the world, isn't it?

*Giving love, receiving love. Being useful.*

Never be afraid to find yourself *in debt* without knowing how you can *repay it.* Give others a chance to love you. To help you, to take care of you. It is not you who desperately ask for it, they are the one who offers themselves, it is time to accept them. Don't be Batman, *the hero that no one wants but that everyone needs*: make room in your heart.

**It is up to you to make others love you.**

Today you give someone a chance to love you. And if there is no one there, make a phone call to someone you would like closer to you.

Write a message to the person you would like by your side, send a simple voice message.

Take the first step. Whatever it is. You have nothing to lose, I swear.

It seems to contradict what I told you in the previous chapter, doesn't it? It is not. Here it is not you who *hide your desire to be appreciated* under the guise of a co-dependency. Here you deliberately ask for a hand, a support, a shoulder. And this healthy step is the first towards an authentic relationship. All authentic relationships. This will give you the strength to surround yourself with people who can see your dream, believe in you and you can believe in them. People who have the will and strength to accomplish the impossible because as Gleen Hefley said: "Every day someone is doing something that someone else thought impossible."

Every day, every moment. You can be one of those people, but you have to believe in yourself and who is next to you. You have to trust those who want to fight with you, not dragging people along for the sole purpose of filling your life. Don't spend your time with people you think are problematic, in trouble, just because you can devote yourself to them without having to work on your goals. Do not tie to your ankle a weight solely to feel justified if instead of running, you walk; free yourself, start to gain speed and share the road with those who go or would like to go in the same direction. Continue this journey alone, but do not push others away, be brave. Show off your courage; you will see it and the others will see it. And nothing will be impossible.

**You are your superhero. You are Superman or Wonder Woman**

# ABOUT CHANCES

For a moment, stop worrying. Today you can take a break and it doesn't matter if it is a difficult time. If it hasn't worked in years. In fact, better this way. If you are there trying and trying again, and you don't even remember when you started, forget it. Stop. I have no doubt that you did your best, I could bet on it. I know you bought all the tools, you updated, you took all the necessary courses, you put all the energy into it, testing your ability in a thousand and many different ways. I know you did, don't despair if it doesn't work. If you have had yourself a motivational speech a billion times, if you have repeated it to your image in the mirror for I don't know how many mornings, if you told yourself you were going to leave, if you forced yourself to come back, if you packed your bags and unpacked them. How much time you spent searching for a solution without finding it: you approached the problem, then you walked away, hoping to see that something you couldn't ever grasp. But again, without success. You have been studying for years, you have fallen asleep on the same book countless times, or you haven't slept in years, you have tried, tried, experimented, you have done more than you ever imagined, you have believed in it more than you thought you could. Stop and smile. You are here. Where? In front of reality. The door in front of you you try to open in every possible way does not have the lock.

*It won't open, it never will open.*

Why?

**Because it is not your door.**

And it is not your fault!

**Repeat with me, "It is not my fault."**

There are things that go beyond our control, things not part of our destiny, things that are not made for us. And we don't have to feel the Guilt. Nor if that story didn't work out. Nor if that job didn't go the way we wanted it to. Nor if a friend has not been faithful. We don't have to feel the weight of Guilt.

And you know why? **Do you know what Guilt is?**
**The most effective leash in the world.**

That leash which is stuck to the door, and you are there waiting. You are waiting in front of a closed door. A door behind which there is nothing at all. And yet you are still there, you are there and you have been there for too long. Well, I'm happy for you because this is your last day.

*Enjoy it.*

Why enjoy it? Because every time you choose you are giving up something, remember? We said at the beginning of our journey you should make waivers, even when the choice you made is the best for yourself. And you, today, giving up your leash and your closed door, you are giving up a lot, a lot.

You are putting your habits aside; you are about to change the land-scape, you will have to invent a new way of life because you will not stand in front of *that door that doesn't open.* Your actions will have an effect again, every gesture a reaction, you will no longer be in front of a wall. Here, for everything you give up, you shall earn another: if you have so much to lose, you also have a lot to gain and what you find you will like.

A few meters ahead, a few meters away, there is your door. The one with the lock, for which you even have the key. The door you are made for, the one that is the size of your dreams. Open it. You will find me on the other side.

*But who and what are these doors?*

Often the door in front of us represents a goal, perhaps what our fam-ily has designed for us, but that does not belong to us. Other times the door is a relationship that has turned into rust and does not allow us to carry on in our lives.

*It can happen, however, that the door that does not open is a person.*

We are in front of them and we are uncomfortable. Have you ever noticed that feeling? They are there telling us about being sick, cry-ing or despairing and we feel discomfort as they show off all their an-ger or sadness. A little voice might pop up inside your head. A little voice that would not give you a break until you *solved* the problem. If so, if this is your case, know that you are trying to solve much more. You are trying *to solve* that person. And by doing so, you are trying *to solve* yourself. You are doing a useful action, you are going to tell me, you are doing good, you are trying to help someone. Your intentions are good. But you are doing it to satisfy your ego, that doesn't feel reasons, to where if the other person - the one you didn't want to do anything but help - didn't take note of your advice and didn't want to apply it, you'd be in trouble. It would bother you; you would not understand and you would ask yourself, "But how is it possible? Why me that I did so much to help them? Just me that I did so much to be close to them?" yes, but so much for whom? So close to whom? The discomfort in which the other people live is unbearable to you. That discomfort blocks you, puts you in trouble and you want to do something - and you would be ready for anything - to solve the problem for the other. Because when a child they told you not to cry because *nothing* had really happened, they told you that crying *is not good* or that you should not cry otherwise others would hear you, that you were making a *fuss*, that continuing like this would make your mother *cry* as well. As if crying was wrong, as if expressing your discomfort was the last thing in the world to do, isn't it? They taught you to Fear emotions, to repress them, there are positive emotions to be shared and others that need to be kept hidden, because they are antisocial, uncomfortable, cumbersome. You cannot accept the discomfort, the pain, the anger, the frustration and seeing them in the eyes of others and it becomes unbearable, as if you were the one feeling them.

# SOMETIMES YOU WANT TO HELP SOMEONE JUST BECAUSE YOU CAN'T ACCEPT THE PAIN OF OTHERS.

Who could blame you?

No one has ever told you that all this is wrong, no one has ever tried to explain to you to accept emotions and you fell into this web too. Now you are part of the ranks of those looking for a way to *fight* or even erase the suffering of Others. Because, we've said this so often, first, you cancel yours.

And then try to solve the problem, whatever it is, as quickly as possible. But not out of altruism, no. To drive away the emotions you are feeling. In doing so, you will never accept your emotions. But it is important. Why? Because those are your emotions, you have to live them, face them, cope with them. Because those are your own emotions thence those emotions are beautiful.

*Your emotions are beautiful.*

And they help you with strategy.

# IT IS NOT THAT IT IS NOT WORKING, IT JUST STILL DOESN'T WORK.

When it comes to achieving your goals, how often have you changed your strategy? You keep doing it. To look for different, innovative solutions, you surprise yourself in comparing your success and your life to Others'. You put your own successes and Others 'on the same scale and wait for the response with anxiety. You look at everything they do, trying to understand. Remember that *understanding* differs greatly from *believing*. And for you, to believe is much more important than to understand: stealing tricks, learning the job, drawing inspiration from Others 'experiences can be useful, but never how much it is to believe in what you do. Whether you are trying or being followed by someone who does my same job - maybe it is the Dream Mentor, the best of them all - what you are doing is always right 99% plus 1%. What are these percentages? Simple: 99% you are doing the right thing because you believe it, at 1% because it is the right choice at the right time. Why?

*Because there are no right choices, no better roads.*

There is only giving the maximum - and therefore getting the most out of it - from the path you are taking. Showing the utmost dedication to your struggle is the best thing you can do, the one that will almost always make it perfect and just. Then you just need a little luck; Steve Job used to say, "More than half the way that separates people from success is perseverance." And the same do I say. Trust yourself, try with all yourself, do not spare yourself, your way can - and will have to - change another thousand times, if a thousand times you realize that you are not happy. Because remember nothing is better than what makes you feel good. Changing can be the solution but only after you have tried them all and put all the effort you could. You owe it to yourself; it is respect for your dreams. Do you remember what you were doing with the wrong door? That is it, but this time your motivations are real and your perseverance will help you. If you throw everything away every time, if you just need an unexpected event to change your mind, if you change your plans once a week, if you question each choice more than once a month you are just feeding your Fears. You give up the fatigue, to anxiety, to Others 'judgment and you change because it is not going well enough, you are not *earning* enough with this method... But you must know this:

**You didn't really change your mind because you were unhappy, you didn't subvert everything because you are unsatisfied, you are trying a new way again because you are afraid.**

Afraid to succeed, sometimes, afraid of failure and having to start again, other times. Then better start again. If you are near the finish line you can start from scratch, get away from your goal and relive the same comfortable steps that took you there. If you are close to failure you will avoid the pain, you will not experience frustration and you can move forward (perhaps stalling) with no shock. But you didn't get involved, you didn't trust yourself and your will. You succumbed to Fear, and *you know what the face of Fear is?* That of an imbecile relative, racist, superficial and extra talkative, of those who ruin the holidays to everyone and who, no reason why, everyone keeps inviting and you find it in front when you should just be happy. That stupid relative who you are carrying around with you and trying to ruin your life, who convinces you to think about success in terms of days instead of years. Who convinces you to think about life in terms of money, when life, emotions, results, love, everything that really matters need time. Time for the conditions to be built, time for the conditions to be created, time for things to happen, to stabilise. Instead, that relative of yours repeats unpleasant phrases like, "That child, at his age, if he is not walking still, he has a problem" and you look at that child and believe in it, you worry about it, maybe he is your son and everything you imagined for him disappears. Or he could tell you "Your cousin will become the youngest student in her category to win that award, she is your age if I'm not mistaken" and you'll count the years you are missing from graduation, going through the awards you have never had, thinking about competitions you have never participated in. "How come you don't see that girl anymore? she was too beautiful for someone like you, you let her get away?" and instead of punching him, you go home, drink, get angry and in despair just to wake up in the morning with a single thought. "I'm not worth anything," you repeat as soon as you open your eyes.

Fear is that relative you should avoid, the one who says stupid, false, bad things, the one who does it on purpose to get you feeling ill-at-ease, uncomfortable, into trouble.

What you are doing is right, I am telling you. Your dream is right because it is your dream. Your goal is the best there can be for you. Because it is not true that it is not working. It just doesn't work yet, but it will work. Like every beautiful thing. Don't forget that.

# DON'T BELIEVE IT IS NOT THE RIGHT TIME. THE RIGHT TIME DOESN'T EXIST. NOW IS THE RIGHT TIME. THE RIGHT TIME IS NOW.

# ABOUT GUILT

We have mentioned Guilt several times, now it is time to delve into the subject.

To do so, I confronted for a long time with one of my dearest friends, that could do nothing else in life than the psychologist and the psychotherapist: **Dr. Enrico Bellucci**, Roman, exceptional professional and great lover of the *Queen*. Many of the concepts explained in this chapter I attribute to the calmness, patience and generosity that Enrico has used unreservedly to guide me on the path of understanding towards the sacred monster, that it is precisely the **Guilt**.

These pages will be of the utmost relevance and I assure you you will feel much lighter, once you reach the end.

In all previous chapters, *Guilt* appeared as an accomplice in behaviours, actions and harmful and dangerous thoughts. Guilt is Public Enemy Number One. Guilt is the biggest obstacle between you and your happiness. Why? Guilt is an emotion, but is it like Fear, love or hunger? No, those are instinctive emotions that come with us. Already a newborn child experiences them in front of the face of the mother or that of a stranger, when maybe it cries because of hunger. Guilt, on the other hand, belongs to a second category of emotions, those induced from the outside: from contact with parents, with school, with religion and with society.

## In a way, we are educated to Guilt.

What? In a simple and almost invisible way.

"Eat everything because there are children who have nothing", "The teacher said you couldn't answer, it is your fault", "Keep an eye on your brother, if something happens it will be on you", "Don't do it anymore, otherwise Dad gets angry". These are more or less familiar phrases. Because as children they tell us we must not make mistakes, that mistakes lead to terrible consequences and terrible consequences generate Guilt. In your mind as a child, associations have been born between what is right and what is not, logical patterns you still carry with you by tying error to punishment, then to suffering and Guilt. A rock that rolls to the bottom of the sea, that is how you feel: dragged down a slope too steep, swallowed by the deep sea, you fall without doing anything. Like it is a fault, a fault of yours. This is a dangerous side effect.

## Being wrong doesn't mean you have a fault.

This phrase should be learned by heart, replacing what we have assimilated over the years, especially in school, where a mistake meant a bad mark. And this negative mark set off repercussions: the disappointed teacher, the angry and suffering parents because of ours and so on. The rock rolls again, it never stops. Instead, you have to stop it. To experience Guilt, to realize that you have not done what you wanted is an important feeling. It allows us to realise our actions, it is fundamental for us and it has been fundamental to human evolution: Guilt is linked to social morality and individual ethics, can we imagine our world without these references? It would be a world of barbarism and inhumane acts. Then Guilt is not born as something unhealthy, but it becomes it. And how? When? The moment when instead of representing a compass of our behaviour becomes a very heavy boulder that blocks the road and paralyses us.

Every gesture, every action, every thought terrifies you. It scares you, the idea of making mistakes, of disappointing, of breaking the expectations of parents, friends or yourself, relentless judge. Then here the Guilt has become too great, it is not born *after* but lives *before* you. No longer after your action, but before it: before you even do something, you already know that it will be all your fault, that whatever goes wrong will be because of you, that every mistake will be because of you and that every criticism, judgment, analysis will be made against you.

**Let's pretend it is all your fault.**

All right, but let's try to change the words. We have already seen how, talking about *the past* and *the future*, the couple, Others 'opinion, just replacing some words make reality less scary and simpler and everything falls into place. I assure you we will do the same with *Guilt*. In fact, let's not call it that anymore. Let's give the blame another name: let's call it *responsibility.*

**Everything happening to you, is your responsibility**

But instead of taking this as the direct shuttle to despair you can think of it in a totally different way. It is no longer a fault, it is no longer something related to a mistake, it is no longer something that lives outside of you: you see, there is no rock rolling down the slope and then sinking. If everything is your responsibility it means you have full control of everything. You have 100% control and you can do, get, achieve whatever you want.

*But why doesn't it work?*
Because you are not in control at all.

At the moment, you share responsibility between yourself and Others, and if you are lucky you give yourself 50%, but the partition will probably not be fair at all, you are unlikely to split the responsibilities in half. Often you leave others a much larger portion of the loot. We saw that, didn't we? Taking control is all you need, not in the unhealthy way we talked about a few chapters ago (when you were probably a completely different person than now), in the desperate quest not to make the unexpected happen, no. Control as a fair sense of responsibility affecting only your actions: knowing that everything depends on you.

*Because should not your actions be your own responsibility, do you know what shall happen?*

You feel resentment, anger, jealousy, envy because others haven't done, don't and won't do what you would have liked. Pull the reins of the horse, don't let others carry you. Because others can't know where you want to go, how you want to get there and what way you would like to follow. Because Others, even if you don't believe it, always do their best. Each of us does the best. All the time. What just seems enough or even wrong to you is the best for someone else.

**We know with what ferocity you judge yourself, the metre is the same one you use to judge Others. No mercy.**

But you can stop, you must do it. You can start at any moment to finally feel compassion and empathy, not to envy someone you think is richer, luckier, more beautiful, more famous than you. You can decide to change your role in the story and the story, you will see, will change.

# THE EXECUTIONER IS ALWAYS TO BLAME. THE VICTIM IS ALWAYS RIGHT.

Guilt, when it takes control of everything belongs to us, drives us to react to limit the damage. But sometimes it becomes a mask behind which to hide by wearing the comfortable clothes of the victim. Think about it, which character is easier to play? Remember, we talked about it earlier.

The victim, the one who always has the audience on its side, for whom everyone moves trying to bring it to the happy ending. A happy ending that is always there, immersed in the compassion of others. What is more, doing nothing, absolutely nothing. Responsibility becomes progressively others'. Here we are in the victim shoes waiting for the cruel fate by continuing to repeat that others are unjust, that they do not do what they should, that do not make us happy, but at the same time - at least at the beginning - we are surrounded by those who will do their best for us, will devote all their own and all their energies. Because they will believe in us, in our suffering, they will think that we are doing our best and that we really need help to get up and continue. No one will notice that we have actually been standing still for quite a while. And then? Then, should that mask fall - and I assure you sooner or later it will happen - we would find ourselves alone. Then we still blame Others, irreconcilable and selfish, when the responsibility is once again ours. Even doing nothing, abandoning the reins and hoping that the horse knows the way, is a choice. Even watching the rock rolling down is choosing.

*You chose, but you made the wrong choice.*

Relying on Fear, Guilt, staying in the victim shoes doesn't work. Never.

**Having made a mistake is nothing more than the certainty you have tried.**

You are a human being, thence your abilities face physiological limits. Remember? You have no control over things, you have control only over yourself and therefore only responsibility for *your* actions.

**Doing the Best you can is the Best you can do.**

*This applies to you, but it also applies to Others.*
Finding the balance between responsibility, control and Guilt is important; "I hurt my friend, I feel Guilty" is not a phrase to be demonized. If you acted regarding your being, if you did your best, if your intentions were good, if you considered that your friend was not like

you, you should not feel Guilty. You can explain yourself, reach out to you again, apologize, but stay free of anguish. Guilt only identifies a discrepancy between our intentions and the effect of actions, not to make us Guilty and to force us to do *everything* we can or could to make up for them.

But Guilt is not only an emotion you feel, you can also teach it. Paying attention to how particular concepts are expressed can help us in children upbringing, in the confrontation with a life partner and can also be a way to verify how much we ourselves are victims of this *perversion* (because this is what it is). For example, trying to convey a concept like "Don't waste food" is definitely a laudable gesture. Nothing is wrong with wanting to share with others a lifestyle we consider - rightly or not, but it is always related to ourselves - just and correct.

"Don't waste food" is a concept.
"Don't waste food because in Africa, children cannot eat" is bullshit.

There is no need to use a comparison to make the idea *more effective*, indeed it is precisely this excess of sense that opens the way to Guilt development. Guilt about *Africa* is being associated with *waste*. To an adult mind, raised without the obsession of Guilt, this is clearly an association that is non-existent, but in children, or in a very sensitive person, it can trigger excessive anxiety, Fear, load of unnecessary responsibilities. The child, for example, might think it *is its fault* if other children do not eat in Africa. Seeds of this kind can settle in the mind and become very dangerous bombs.

**Combining *right* actions and *wrong* contexts creates Guilt.**

Your parents didn't do it on purpose, as they were definitely raised like that. Forgive them. Do no longer pay the consequences of this *upbringing misbehaviour*. Guilt is an octopus with long tentacles, a monster with long arms. It is inside you and it contaminates everything, feeding on your Fears. The first conviction we questioned was about the past, remember? The past doesn't exist. It may have seemed like a random choice, but it is not. The past is the place where our Fears have been nourished and Fears are the most favourite food of Guilt. Regrets arise from there and chain us, paralyse us, having incredible repercussions on our present, even affecting future choices. Because that is how it works: I act, I make a decision, I realise I'm wrong and I feel the regret it is just Guilt with another face. What we have said before is still true: to abandon Guilt, remember that we have done our best. All the time. Even that day two years ago, when we chose to be with a person who today made us suffer, even a week ago when we decided to trust a friend who betrayed us, each time we chose to the best of our ability.

**Remember that Past no longer exists and cannot be changed.**

You just have to accept that you have made the only choice at that time and that doesn't mean you have made a mistake. And if you made no mistake, there is no fault to feed, right?

*Why is Guilt so strong?*

Because it is a leash, it is the most powerful weapon we have and we use it to keep ourselves restrained, that little voice that tells us we could have done more - and that we pander not by giving our energies, but by shrugging our shoulders and declaring that we have already done enough - it helps us to control Others, to condition their choices, it becomes a treacherous mechanism by which to convince others to do something someway and not vice versa. Guilt is the shortest way; it is the tightest rope that binds us to others. But awareness is a boomerang. When you learn to read, you can no longer avoid doing so, so when you become aware of Guilt you can no longer avoid to feel it. If you realize you have tied others to you through Guilt, you won't be able to do that anymore. Because you will finally realise that everything you have done, said, thought, built through Guilt is only an illusion.

**Guilt gives you the illusion of living. Only when you break it does life begin for real.**

Doing it is no small thing, it is not a result achieved without effort or effort. Even just talking and dealing with a subject like *Guilt* is no small feat, I know. Untying it means changing most of your landmarks, really moving your roots. It can be difficult; indeed, it will be. But not enough to give up.

# GUILT IS A BAND, LET IT FINISH PLAYING.

We talked about what Guilt is, now we roll up our sleeves and try to figure it out and finally escort it to the way out.

First, I chose the image of a rope, which binds you and the Others. This is true, but it is also true that Guilt binds ourselves with our being. Then it is also the most gigantic umbilical cord that exists. Why a cord? Because it nourishes, every moment, nonstop, day and night.

*Of poison and resentment and Fear, but it still nourishes.*

And this is the reason it is so hard to live without it, it is an addiction, we are addicted to it and we believe we can't live without it. But it is not your fault they didn't love you enough. If your parents couldn't look after you. It is not your fault someone you loved is gone. If someone betrayed your trust. It is not your fault you can't save everyone. If that person didn't listen to you. It is not your fault if your heart hurts, if you eat because you suffer, if you don't breathe well, if you walk wrong, if you have been teased or hurt or insulted. If that person followed your advice and things didn't work out for them. And you, with your big heart, pay the price for everyone else and your own arms show the scars of their wrong choices. Let go of what doesn't depend and never depended or shall depend on you. *How can you survive with this weight?*

Let go of the Guilt with the convenience it brings: to be certain that whatever you do, you will never be happy and it will never be your fault. The power of your choices is like that of Spider Man (are you a superhero remember?), it is great and big responsibilities come with it. You have to dream big; you have to do the best for yourself. All you have to do is have complete control over your present. And you do.

*But Guilt is a band, isn't it?*

Thence, do you still hear it playing? Is it the singer who voices your Fears? You hear how it screams, it shakes, it raises its voice. Watch it try to pull you close, to force you into Fear. Let it do it. Let the Guilt band be voiceless, you have better things to do than listen to it.

# 7 STEPS AWAY FROM YOUR FREEDOM.

This chapter has been the longest so far because it is the most difficult to deal with. I did not want to leave unexplored any corner of the great monster that is Guilt, to free you from its long tentacles.

*You will make it and I trust you.*
*You will be back doing your best.*
*The target is not as far away as it seems.*

For this reason, I want to briefly summarise the 7 basic steps that separate you from your freedom. See? It is only seven. One step at a time and let's walk away.

1. We learned to call Guilt by its real name: ***responsibility.***

What you think is a fault mixes with your beliefs, but what is there in your past that haunts you so hard? What did you do that leaves you breathless? Taking responsibility is the first and indispensable step: don't stall, act. Don't let any fault to sink you, but make responsibility push you to choices.

2. Reconsider yourself, your values, your rules and your expectations.

We have already said that *expecting* something means disappointment, so enough with expectations, that could be unattainable and frustrating or filled with performance anxiety. Set goals and engage all of yourself to achieve them. What if you don't like something? Change it. And if it is something that is inside you, that is part of your roots? Change that too, it is not impossible. **We are not beings bound to be always the same.** If you don't believe it anymore, if it just makes you sick, maybe it is not right for you anymore, it is not what you want anymore.

3. Manage your displeasure, **control the Fear you have of Others ' judgment**.

Guilt arises from there, from that unhealthy Fear of receiving a rebuke, a scold, just like when you were a child. You don't have to do what you don't like to do, remember? You must not always say *yes* just for the Fear of disappointing others: acting in this way will create Guilt towards yourself and that is not what you want. Believing that people abandon us because we have made a mistake is a chimera and being terrified of making mistakes does not help us: sooner or later, we will fail, if not today it is tomorrow, and that is not why others will abandon us. What if they do? Their choice, it is not your fault. They would have done it anyway. And you can't believe you are never wrong.

4. **You are human, and as such, you can be wrong.**

What you need to worry about is not *if* you are going to be wrong, but *when* you will be, and meanwhile give your best, all the time. Because when you find you are wrong, you are not going to have anything to reproach yourself with. You will be at peace with yourself and also with Others, aware that you have given everything you had, that you have chosen to the best of your ability and that you have been the best version of yourself. Nothing else. We are not machines and, unfortunately, we may make the same mistakes in the same situations, unfortunately, experience does not always work as it should. But it is not a tragedy. We just need to realise it and change actions or change situations to get different results because always doing the same thing, you will always get the same result. Keep it stuck in your head while you forgive yourself.

5. Nothing is as difficult in the world as forgiving.

But listen: is it ever possible to keep the weight of every mistake you make on your shoulders forever? No, it is not. Of course not. Your urgency must be to free yourself from the weight of the past, forgive yourself, only so Guilt will deflate. Like a balloon, like an aria of an opera when the breath in the lungs it is over. If you are like Maria Callas it takes a long time, but it is going to end sooner or later. **Forgive yourself.**

6. **And remember that the Past is immutable.**

No matter how great Guilt may be, it won't change things, because the past is the place of what things already happened. Can you change something that has already happened? No, then why fuel Guilt. Repeat to yourself, *"Feeling Guilty won't change* things." Thence, what can you do? Carry on, it is clear. Doing your best, always at every step.

# NO GUILT WILL EVER BE BIG ENOUGH TO CHANGE THE PAST.

7. And now the Last Step, the most important one.

A concept I have been insisting on since the beginning of this journey

**Build your happiness by agreeing to deserve it.**

To fight Fear, to overcome Guilt, nothing is better than to feed no longer with anxieties and Fears, but knowing that we deserve the best. Why? Because you are doing your best, because it is you and you couldn't be better than what you are. I'm telling you. You deserve every success, you deserve to win the races you face, you deserve to get that degree, to get that job, to be loved by your children and parents, to be appreciated by your employees. You have nothing wrong, absolutely nothing.

the guilt is a long tentacle octopus a monster with long arms

# ABOUT FEAR

You are here on this cliff and you are not afraid of heights. The sun is high and the light is clear. The sea below you is soft and full of colors, so bright and beautiful that you want everything but to remain where you are. Feel the precipice creak under your feet, then close your eyes and open your *arms. Breathe.* Go back with your memory to the last time you felt so free. Fix that point. Don't get distracted, look at it carefully. Don't let it go, breathe in it. Smell it. Here, now you are ready. Dive!

## THE EMOTION THAT LASTS LONGER, LASTS ONLY 90 SECONDS.

Are you still afraid to let go? Do you feel that the height is too much for you? Breathe again and listen to me. The Fear you feel, if you will stay still there, will last forever because Fear is an emotion that if you don't let go, if you don't face it, it lasts forever. But do you know how long an emotion lasts on average? A few hours? A few days? None of this. You'd be surprised to find that it hardly exceeds the minute.

That is right: **what you are feeling, it is already passed.**

The Fear of flight, the adrenaline of jumping, the terror of empti-ness, everything will last less than the fall. Amazing, isn't it? That is just the way it is. **Emotions pass through the body between 6 and 90 seconds:** anger is the one that lasts the longest, which influences us the longest. Everything else? Just a moment and nothing more. The clock hand ticking and it is already over. And you thought the emotions lasted for hours, days, maybe years. Because That is what we are used to believing: that we will be in love forever, that gratitude is eternal, that pain will never go away, that that person will be angry with us all their life. That is not the case. So, if the emotions don't last that long what is inside us? What gets stuck in us? Nothing. It is just you who think you are a prisoner of your emotions, but now you know you have got all the right skills to free yourself. Think of the very small children and how they change their mood, in a blink of an eye, in a rapid and unpredictable way: they go from joy to despair in a second then return to rejoice after a moment more. Don't they feel real emotions? No, their emotions are as true as yours. Then why are they acting like this? Because emotions go through their little bodies in a few moments and there is no trace of them. See? Emotions last a moment, it is just the memory, memories and experience that ampli-fy them over time. In fact, as the baby grows up, it will sulk longer, it will be whimsical, and it will cry often because it will have learned. Here is the experience that plays its role, that if they cry, they will have more attention.

**Tears do not continue along with suffering but with need.**

But children are free from Fear and then they don't need to make you feel Guilty. They don't hold grudges. They don't need to make you understand that they love you; otherwise, you won't love them back. *At least for a while,* until education takes its course, and the same mechanisms that have trapped you will besiege them too. But remember that you were that child too, and you can learn a lot from them. They can help you remember that when you talk about your pain as if it was there with you at that moment, it is actually already passed. If you feel anger, like it is in your heart, and you can't help but spit it out of your chest, it is actually already over. Your love for that person, the disappointment for their estrangement, the embarrassment and shame you felt because you think it was your fault, they haven't existed for months. It is not there with you anymore, and you don't have to pretend it is there. It is not by being surrounded by ghost emotions you will find happiness.

*But if those emotions don't exist, what does?*

This.
**This precise, unique, only moment.**

And you, who live it (in this case with me). And the things that happened to you don't have to affect what you do and what you think. You can't get caged, you don't deserve it, and it wouldn't be fair. You don't have to give emotions control, as we've already decided that you won't entrust it to Others. And now these sentences, they make a lot more sense than when we talked about it at the beginning of the book, don't they? Because even the noblest or most horrible of emotions lasts at most a stupid minute and a half. Everything else is fabricated by you, to feel like you exist. Because you think that by prolonging your anger you will tell the world and yourself that you are *really* angry. Because as you continue to show your surprise, you can scream to the world and in the mirror you have been really surprised.

You dilute drops of emotion into litres of water to prove that you have lived, that you are living. That you exist.

*And to exist sometimes, you just want to suffer.*

But it only lasts a moment, there is nothing to fear. And why do you want to pay the price for a lifetime?

**Do you want to be afraid forever?**

As despair envelops you, remember one thing: suffering, for you, is still easier to accept than to be afraid. You are blocking yourself; you are limiting your chances, you are closing out the window the chance to be happy. Everything you are doing to question yourself, your choices, the person you have next door or who you choose not to have next door, your parents, your job, in summary, everything, is based on Fear. The Fear of losing. The Fear of public humiliation. The Fear of making mistakes, failing, disappointing. The Fear of not being enough for someone or anyone at all. The Fear of something that does not exist and will never exist keeps you still at a point of time where nothing bad has yet happened. Remember? The future doesn't exist, it is just a fantasy. A powerful fantasy that scares you. And what makes you so afraid? It makes you run away or stand still, pushes you back or paralyzes you. It breaks your breath, twists your stomach, twists your neck and takes your sleep off. There is nothing but that Fear, a single black emotion that overwhelms everything else: you are no longer there, there is only Fear in your place. That doesn't make you go half an inch forward, forward to something you want and that you think you don't deserve at all. Because Fears have turned into certainties: you are not enough, you are not worth enough, they are no longer doubts but certainties. And who certified them if not Fear itself? But you hide because you don't want to suffer and tell yourself it wasn't the right job, the right opportunity, the right man or woman for you. That was not the time, that then the opportunity will come. You tell yourself that you are busy, too much work, too much bad luck, too many difficulties to overcome and you tell yourself that

*"Why should I do it?"*

**Because it is you who will make it**, because you can fight it this Fear and it is a sign you can already get where you want.

*You only have one huge handbrake pulled.*

Who will not make it is not those who is paralyzed in terror, but those who do not even feel afraid at all. If you know you are terrified, if you admit it to yourself, you are already one step ahead. If you don't hide, you can seize life again. We've seen it, the excitement lasts a few moments, and instead, you will live much longer than that. You have a whole life ahead of you, your new life, a second part: the one that starts now and starts with one step, towards everything you want.

**Whatever it is, take the first step. Do it with me.**

Do not replace Fear with indifference or apathy or surrender. It is not tiredness that is going to win you over. It won't be another excuse, another blanket pulled up over your head to hide. Live this Fear for what it is, allow yourself to feel it. Then it passes, I swear.

*Trust me once again.*

Remember that suffering so as not to admit that you are afraid is not courage, but a shortcut. You don't show any attachment to life, you are not fighting for your happiness if you are telling lies. Don't give up, it is hard I know, but you are not alone. And the love you deserve is infinite; the joy you deserve in life, in relationships, in work, is infinite.

**Just as infinite your heart and your capacity to love are.**

Breathe and start walking. I'm here with you, I will always accompany you.

*My grandfather, Air Marshal during World War II, use to tell his daughter, my mother: "When you are afraid, think of your father. Your father, who at sunset, in spite of everything, pointed towards the horizon and landed."*

# ABOUT THE STORM THAT WILL COME

Sometimes, you even struggle to think. There is a dull noise in the head. A constant muttering. Feel the water get to your ankles, then reach your waist and finally get to your shoulders. Thinking of anything other than water that keeps going up is impossible. The others talk, but you don't listen to them. The Others ask, but you don't answer. Things happen, but you are not there. You are not here with them; you are not here with you. You are alone with water at your throat. You can't even concentrate because you are struggling to breathe. Then you hear a new noise, somewhere else, that resonates in your body and bounces inside you. You don't know where it is coming from, you don't know what it is, but you feel like something is in you. You feel like something inside you is broken and you have no glue, no hands, no love to put it back together. You look inside yourself and you see that fracture, that subtle gap in which doubts, insecurities, sufferings are. You try to hold it together, but another spike and the wound opens, something else breaks. See the scaffolding creak and lose pieces, but you can do nothing about it. You don't even know where to start. And That is how things happen, don't give in to displeasure or frustration. Don't give up because the past doesn't define you in any way, not even the person you were 10 minutes ago defines you anymore. They no longer define you for mistakes, misunderstandings, suffering. Those wounds that open, those parts of

you that break and collapse, must fall. Let them do it, even if it is not easy to stay in place when everything seems to go wrong.
*This is where you have to be.*

Even if it hurts, you have to pass through here. From this feeling of defeat, from the impression of being in the midst of a sea of "I will never make it" "Everything is too difficult" and «I don't have the strength". Don't think you have been unlucky, that you have gone the wrong way, that hellfire is going to overwhelm you. If the flames burn out and everything is lost, think you'll finally have a clear view looking out of your windows. Just what you needed. Because what happens to you has a lot more to do with what you want than you think. You have to trust yourself.

*A lot more than you are giving yourself now.*

Because you got here on your own, with your legs, with your thoughts, with your courage. Whatever you are facing if you feel it is falling apart is because you need it to fall apart. And start again. Be patient, it is not forever. Nothing is forever in this world.

*And even if this seems like hell to you, you are in pieces, in billions of drops of water, you are storm.'*

You can put out the fire and give birth to life. Like a phoenix. The fire burns, but you are not firewood, you are spark, you are master of the flames, you are the flames. Like a phoenix reborn from its ashes, you will be reborn. Stronger. More beautiful, like that.

# PEOPLE WILL TELL YOU THAT YOU WILL NOT OVERCOME THE STORM BUT YOU WON'T CARE, PEOPLE DON'T KNOW YOU ARE THE STORM.

Do not listen to those who will not trust you, to all those who will do nothing but shout "Fire, fire!", all those who will tell you to run away. That you can't make it past this moment, this event, this thing. You have put aside your dreams and goals so often that you don't even know who you are anymore, not even who you are. You have forgotten the most important thing of all, your only truth, the one you should cherish as the most precious gift in the world. And I don't know why anyone didn't believe in you, but why you, in the first place, made nothing but make excuses. You are the one who stopped believing in yourself, you saw the flames and you were afraid. You heard the storm and ran straight away to close the windows. You opened the front door to anyone, asked for help from every possible person, and even accepted the advice of strangers rather than listening to what you had to say about your own thoughts. How can the phoenix be reborn if it Fears its own ashes? If you give others the freedom to throw it away, why is it only dust?

*Can you imagine a phoenix without self-confidence?*
*Who dies saying, "Oh, let's hope it is going to end well this time as well..."?*

You tried, I know, but then you raised your arms giving up because of a rejection or a handful of *no, thank you.* And that was it.

Repeat with me:

*how many more times am I going to give up my life?*
**None more.**
*How many more times do I plan to give up before I start?*
**None more**
*How many more times do I want to convince myself that I'm doing enough when I'm not doing anything?*
**None more.**

### Your sole, unique, concern is to be happy.

Success means happiness. And to succeed you have to try, you have to make mistakes, you have to fail. No man has ever lived without mistakes, no man has crossed this world without collecting a few things to be ashamed of.

### The only person in the world who never makes a mistake is the one who never tried, someone said.

And if in the last hour, on the last day, in the last week, you did nothing that went into that direction and well, you, my friend, you are throwing your life away. Literally. By sacrificing it on the altar of generosity or insecurity, you are throwing your life into Fear, you are trading it for a little peace, for a few thoughts less, for a little security more. But how long does this stability last? One moment, at the next shock, at the next gust of wind, you will be even more afraid. And you will be more and more unhappy and poor. Any compromise will be more difficult, worn out. Until you have nothing left to sacrifice. So, what are you going to do? Will you find the strength to leave or will you remain glued to your place? Because I assure you you will have endless days and chances to succeed if you only try, but you will have no chance if you decide to stay where you are. Only those who buy the ticket have the chance to win the lottery and it makes no sense to curse the good luck of the winner if you have done nothing but assist without participating.

*Don't stand by and watch* **No more.**
*Start over, now, immediately.*
**With everything you have got.**

And if someone, or you, says you are not enough, answer that **not only are you enough, but that you are everything.**

And you have the stubbornness to get there. Wherever you want.

**Despite everything.**
**Thanks to everything.**

# TRUST YOUR HEART ONLY.

So far, you have followed me all the way here, but I know there is going to be a time when your legs will hurt if it hasn't already arrived. That moment when you are going to think that "everything is beautiful, but I can't do it." And you will want to give up.

There will come a time when, right in the middle of fatigue and ascent, when you are putting all the effort in the world into taking back your life, someone will say to you," That is the way you are, you did it that way because..." and you will find yourself thinking *That is not true.* You'll find yourself looking all the way down and cursing against what they know of you by saying, "*All this effort not to be understood?*"

Well, you will probably think you are doing something wrong, or you will get a lot of excuses and alibis, you will say you don't have to prove anything to anyone anymore. That is okay. But the fatigue will be sneaky and those phrases instead of pushing you to continue, to make an additional effort, will make you stop. There will come a time when reason, commitment and fatigue will leave the place to Fear, again. And you are going again to leave to it the reins of your decision.

*Again, again.*
It doesn't matter if you have already fallen for it or if it is the first time you have pulled the oars in the boat, it doesn't matter. Fear doesn't make discounts. It takes command of your ship and you end up straight into the sea, on a run-down raft and without rum. At that point, you start sailing without following the route, without listening to what you want, without reckoning with your real desires, with your chances of being happy.

*And it is just a matter of merit: that you are not going to give yourself.*

You are the captain of the ship, not just a sailor, let alone a passenger that is onboard without even knowing why. You are not the spectator of the game, you are the player, the star of the team. Take your place again. You are not walking on a slab of ice, no more, at a point in time That is no longer this maybe, but not today. You have stuck in the past or you have stuck in the predictions of the future. But not now.

*You are gone at that point.*

You are only there because you are not letting your heart speak. The only one who should always have time and space to express itself, the only one you should always pay attention to.

The only one you can trust.
*And I speak with its voice.*

There is no Fear here, there is no pain, no judgment. Take all the words and let them go through him, focus on the heartbeat and take your breath away.

**Let yourself be guided and trust**
There is no one who knows you better than it does. No one who knows you better than yourself

Then when the time of fatigue and despondency comes, you will know that that moment is the only one that really matters, neither the one before nor the next, and you will continue the journey.

*Again, always, next to your heart, on your legs.*

# JUST BEGIN, IT COULD BE SUCH AN UNEXPECTED SUCCESS

We've come to the end of our trip together, but I still have something to tell you.

In these pages, I have repeated to you several times that finding your freedom, detaching yourself from all Fears and constraints, is the only way to happiness. But what is this happiness, but being yourself? I know this isn't the first time you have heard similar reflections, but give me a few more minutes of your time. You may have found yourself smiling as you read these pages, you will have been saddened by acknowledging your behaviors, you will have nodded, you will have thought "it is true", you will have said I would like to do so", but the Fear may be even greater than you.

Follow me then, let's go give it a good kick whenever it needs us to.

# ABOUT THE IMPORTANCE OF BREATHING

These are the last pages together and saying goodbye hurts me now.

Then I want you not to feel as bad as I do.

Look at your shoulders: I think they are high and stiff, stuck.
When you breathe little, because you give yourself a tiny breath of air and nothing more, your shoulders get up and down.

Up and down.

If you focus for a few seconds, you may find out how painful this movement is. It all comes from that constant stiffness of the shoulders, from that abdomen that does not swell.

Look at it, turn your attention to your navel, what do you wear?
It does not move, does not follow the natural rhythm of breathing?

But it is clear, because you don't breathe.

And you probably find yourself pulling your belly inwards, as if you are ashamed. In fact, you are ashamed.

How many horrendous things we have discovered just by looking at this gesture, as natural as breathing is. How bad you do to yourself and what bad thoughts you cultivate about yourself.

We found them in a gesture that should be the most beautiful, calming and delicate in the world, just as powerful and regenerating: breathing. But you don't breathe.

Do not breathe because you walk on the tips, not to disturb, not to be observed, to go unnoticed and hide your presence from the world and Others. And you can't scream, even if you want to, because there is not enough air inside your lungs and it would take too much: you don't have any, you never had any. Because they taught you to keep your belly backwards. Who? All your secret viewers who watch you, watch you and judge you. Who are they? The first is you, precisely you.

**But you have to breathe.**
**You have to breathe.**

Because if you don't start with that, you will come back tonight with a sore body and a mind destroyed by fatigue. With a worn body and mind there is nothing you can do and instead, there is something wonderful to recover. There is something beautiful about you we went to get in these pages. There are your unique choices, your perfect thoughts, there is you, over every possible person in the world: and there is only one copy of you.

*Unique, inimitable, unrepeatable.*

Do you understand how important this is? And if it is not for Others, it doesn't matter. It has to be for you. Because that is where it starts, from your affection, from your love, from your consideration. Only this is in your power, that is your responsibility alone. Then the rest will go to its place, trust me.

*And now close your eyes.*

Take a deep breath, push the air inside you and if you feel it hurts, insist. Now is the time to continue. What hurts is the air that GOES IN corners of your lungs where oxygen has been missing for years.

*Now you can push it out.*

Do it again.

*Three breaths; start with three breaths.*

They are a good start; you don't have to expect too much from your body. You neglected it for a long time and now you have to take care of it. Three is more than enough, an almost magical number, don't you think? You'll get to the rest, but in the meantime, know that you have already changed your day. And to change your life, all you have to do is repeat yourself.
Because what is your whole life but the set of your days?
Start, three breaths at a time. One day at a time.

# BREATHE.

If everything went as it was supposed to go, this book led you to different feelings and sensations: awareness, exaltation, emotion, rediscovery, finally saying, "But it is true!".
But give me a few more pages. A few pages before concluding. Have you noticed that some of the things are all within your reach? In fact,

they are already inside you. I'm sure you found them; you just have to get them out.

Because remember, it is from your day 0 that you already have everything you need to get what you want and be the person you want. It is all hiding somewhere in there.

**You don't need to change anything about yourself, nothing.**
*You don't need to adapt to any situation that makes you sick.*
*You don't need to pander to anyone to feel loved or loved.*

To get there, you don't need to get anywhere, just to accept this truth within you.

*You have to start with what keeps you alive.*

Get rid of everything other than what *really* keeps you alive, what is indispensable to you. Breathe. It seems simple and obvious and yet it is not. You weren't breathing and you had to. You have to breathe again, but with awareness. You have to breathe because it is the action you have been doing all day, every day, since you have been in the world. The first thing you did coming into the world. Screaming, maybe.

**Breathing, your breath has always been with you.** *He has known you forever.*
It broke with your heart as they left you, it screamed with joy with you, it repaired wounds, sewed pieces, warmed hands, blew all your candles, he sighed words of love, of pleading, of hope, he rested on all his lips along with you, on the skin, on your hands. It was there with you at all times, it was and is your life. Your breath, which you

always forget, is with you. He's always been with you and keeps you alive.

Let's practice one more time.

Close your eyes (after you finish reading, otherwise it becomes complicated), focus on your shoulders, they are high, they are stiff, let them go loose. You need to relax. Look for your breath, look at where it fills the ribcage, the centre of the pyramid and focus on that spot. Did you find it? All right and now take control over it.

*Inhale.*
Push that spot out, fill up with air, to the furthest corners of your body.
Wait and count slowly.
Let the breath sediment inside you, let the oxygen look around.

*Exhale.*
The shoulders are lowered, the breath gets deeper.

Open your eyes. You are here. Is it you? There is only one person in the world like you and that person is you. You can't afford to forget that. You can't let anyone destroy it. You can't let anything cancel it. It is you; it is the most precious thing in the world. Keep breathing, at all times. Don't let life overwhelm you and make you lose control. You have to breathe. *Inhale.* Feel the air inside you again. Wait. *Exhale.* Get rid of the weight. And when everything seems to slip away, when everything will appear to your eyes as too big, too strong, too heavy, **you stop and breathe.**
Look at things for what they are: *things.* What about you? Instead, you are the strongest and most important person in the world.

**Because you are here, and you are alive, and it is you.**

And if you continue to see yourself alive, in the perfect miracle that you are, you will never be unhappy again one day, throwing away all anguish with the air you throw out and inhaling every possible opportunity that exists in the world.

# YOU ARE YOUR GIFT.

Well, our journey together has really come to an end. Writing to you was a blessing, I hope I have conveyed to you what I feel and that these words of mine will be for you a point of reference. That stick when you will think you have lost your way again. You were brave in deciding to confront yourself, you were brave if you didn't keep hiding. I'm proud of you, really.

I can't help but thank you. Then thank you. Thank you for coming or going this far. Thank you for reading me and letting you be accompanied. I will always be here, by your side if you need it. You won't be alone anymore.

Thank you, really

Yours
*Bea*

let the breathe lies in you

# ABOUT SPECIAL THANKS

My personal thanks are for my mom and dad, who have never stopped changing for me, for my true and only love: Francesco, who has never stopped looking at me in the eyes and telling me that I'm beautiful and that he is proud of me, even when I do not deserve it.

For Dr. Enrico Bellucci who helped me understand the guilt, for my psychoanalyst Dr. Marco Guadalupi who saved me.

For my masters: Bianca Pitzorno, J.K. Rowling, Italo Calvino and some of their characters as *Prisca*, *Elisa* and *Marcovaldo*, Daniel Pennac, Alessandro Baricco, Giulio Cavalli, Grazia Oggiano, Stefano Benni, (who takes me to the bar with his friends who have now become mine too) and for the people who have always or forever believed in me: Paolo Micanti, Annina Oldini, Federica Micoli, Cristina Fogazzi, Valentina Mavela, Michele Ciambellini.

To all those who listen to me, I owe everything, the good fortune to be seen and heard.
Thank you

Printed in Great Britain
by Amazon